Kristen Welch is a woman who lives and loves with a rare authenticity that's contagious. She knows what it's like to feel weary from the weight of religion and what it's like to fall passionately in love with Jesus in a whole new way. She'll help you do the latter on the pages that follow. Get ready for more mercy, courage, and grace in your life.

HOLLEY GERTH
Bestselling author of *You're Already Amazing*

All of our excuses have met their match. Kristen tells the beautiful story of a God-sized dream called Mercy House, a story that began when Kristen and her family said yes. Read this book and be inspired to stop second-guessing whether your God-sized dream can ever come true. It can. It absolutely can.

DEIDRA RIGGS
Founder, JumpingTandem; managing editor, *The High Calling*

A delightfully honest read for anyone who ever wondered if her small yes matters. Kristen's words will wake you up from the American Dream you never even knew you were sleeping through.

MYQUILLYN SMITH
Author of *The Nesting Place*

Get ready to take a trip back to the time when you used to dream big. Kristen Welch will introduce you to that girl once again. Her journey of faith and daily courage will inspire you. Who knows how this book will change the direction of your life!

ARLENE PELLICANE
Speaker and author of *31 Days to Becoming a Happy Wife*

RHINESTONE JESUS

rhinestone JESUS

SAYING YES TO GOD

*when sparkly, safe faith
is no longer enough*

KRISTEN WELCH

TYNDALE™
MOMENTUM

*An Imprint of
Tyndale House Publishers, Inc.*

Visit Tyndale online at www.tyndale.com.

Visit Tyndale Momentum online at www.tyndalemomentum.com.

Visit the author's website at www.wearethatfamily.com.

TYNDALE is a registered trademark of Tyndale House Publishers, Inc. *Tyndale Momentum* and the Tyndale Momentum logo are trademarks of Tyndale House Publishers, Inc. Tyndale Momentum is an imprint of Tyndale House Publishers, Inc.

Rhinestone Jesus: Saying Yes to God When Sparkly, Safe Faith Is No Longer Enough

Designed by Jennifer Ghionzoli

Edited by Bonne Steffen

Published in association with the literary agency of William K. Jensen Literary Agency, 119 Bampton Court, Eugene, OR 97404.

Library of Congress Cataloging-in-Publication Data

Welch, Kristen.
  Rhinestone Jesus : saying yes to God when sparkly, safe faith is no longer enough / Kristen Welch.
    pages cm
  Includes bibliographical references.
  ISBN 978-1-4143-8942-4 (sc)
  1. Christian women—Religious life. 2. Christian life. I. Title.
  BV4527.W436 2014
  248.8′43—dc23   2014001412

Printed in the United States of America

20	19	18	17	16	15	14
7	6	5	4	3	2	

To Jesus, my rescuer:
These words are for your glory.
And to everyone else brave enough
to say yes to God

CONTENTS

FOREWORD

You can lose your rhinestones, and it can feel like someone just lifted a millstone that's been breaking your neck.

Yeah—lose a rhinestone or two and you lose the rock that's been weighing you down.

Kristen Welch turns a corner in her life and finds her face right up against what she never expected: Was Jesus an accessory to her life? Or the only thing necessary?

This is a story of one woman, one mom, who decided to simply say yes to doing the next thing in front of her—and discovered the startling truth:

Small Yeses to the Next Thing translate to Huge Yeses and New Things in the Kingdom of God.

Changing the world started with changing her words. Instead of saying, "No, I could never do that" she started saying, "Yes, God could even do that—through even me."

It wasn't that she thought she was a woman who could really do something big—but that she really believed God could do anything big with anyone willing.

Kristen and I have sat together several times. I've leaned forward to hear the heartbeat of Jesus in her quiet words. I've heard the tremble in her voice. I've listened to her honest laugh, her understated, brazen vulnerability. I've watched her face tell this story—the story of deciding that she didn't want her life to be about just getting by, just getting through. That's the thing: they say that life's just about putting one step in front of the other. But the real truth is, sometimes there is no way through anymore, no more just taking one step in front of the other. Sometimes the only way through is by taking wild leaps of faith.

I've been captivated by just that in Kristen's life. There's nothing like it—to witness the raw beauty of a woman who really lives into the fullness of wild faith. There is no really living without really saying yes. Without really taking one step that is actually a leap.

There comes a moment in every woman's life when something she was tightly holding on to—just slips from her hands. Sometimes it's a dream. Sometimes it's a place . . . a person . . . a purpose. Sometimes it's the life you always thought you'd be living.

And you find yourself standing in front of the mirror, realizing that the faith you've been pulling on every day doesn't seem to be enough.

What happens when you look yourself right in the eye and realize, *I'm not living like just Jesus is enough for me.*

What happens when you realize that, really? You actually want a lot more than just Jesus.

That's the moment when the rhinestone falls, clatters, across the floor.

That's the moment you find yourself invited into endless diamond fields of real faith.

The actual Kingdom of God.

This book in your hands is your invitation to The Real More.

So the whole Body of Christ could look into the mirror and see it right there in the eyes, in all of our eyes . . .

a shimmer that is genuine Jesus.

Ann Voskamp

Board member for Mercy House Kenya;
author of the *New York Times* bestsellers *One Thousand Gifts:
A Dare to Live Fully Right Where You Are* and *The Greatest Gift*

INTRODUCTION

WE THINK BIG IN TEXAS. When I was in high school, I was ready to change the world for God. I wasn't sure what that was going to look like or exactly how I was going to do it, but I was certain it would happen. People could see I was a Christian because I pinned on my sparkly symbol of faith, my rhinestone "Jesus" pin, nearly every day; my identity was pretty hard to miss. For the most part, I lived up to the ideal, not doing anything that would taint my good-girl reputation.

I met my husband, Terrell, in Bible school. He loved people and had placed his life in God's hands, too, to lead him where he could make the most impact for the Kingdom. Together we took ministry positions in the church, and our family began to grow. And then a series of incidents suddenly made our simple life and sincere dream to make a difference more complicated and increasingly out of our grasp. Some days time flew by and on other days it seemed to stand still. Suddenly I was thirty years old, raising babies and feeling exhausted and tired of life. Terrell was feeling the pressure of providing for our family and struggling with whether the job he had at the church was really the place God wanted him to be.

I was weighed down by sadness because I had stopped dreaming of changing the world for God. I was just trying my best to survive it.

One night Terrell said, "We used to be dreamers. *What happened to us?*"

Well, life happened.

I spent my days wishing for better ones, fantasizing about the future. But I also began second-guessing my worth, my ability to accomplish anything other than dealing with dirty diapers and tackling the mountain of laundry that never seemed to shrink.

And then Terrell helped me begin dreaming again when he brought home a laptop and encouraged me to write. I had always loved telling stories. Jotting down my thoughts helped me process the ups and downs of life, and I believed it was a gift God had given me. It had gotten pushed aside for years, so I was a little rusty. But the stories I had accumulated in my heart were still there. Starting a blog was a relief.

Oh, don't get me wrong. Life wasn't suddenly a fairy tale. There were still a lot of disappointments and hard times ahead. There were days filled with the exhaustion that comes from puke and poop, drama and bad attitudes. There were job changes and financial worries. I went to hell and back in my marriage, and fought my way to love. I was poor; I was rich. I had good intentions and failed. I had given up on my dreams.

But I slowly discovered that God didn't require me to get my act together before He would reveal His God-sized dream; He was just waiting for me to say yes to Him in my mess. I was about to learn that's when His power proves most effective.

Yes, this is my story of a discarded dream that was restored.

But it's also permission for you to dream again. I hope you will also be inspired to think about offering God the gift of your yes, no matter how big or small or messy it may seem. At the end of each chapter under the heading "Unpinned Faith" I've included some reflections and personal challenges for you. Why "unpinned faith"? I spent my first thirty-seven years wearing my sparkly, pinned-on faith and trying to fit Jesus into my life. It wasn't until I started *fitting my life into Jesus* that my faith became enough. Saying yes to Him has led me on an unbelievable journey.

So . . .

> *if you have a dream*
> *if you have stopped dreaming*
> *if you need more time*
> *if you have too much time*
> *if you want to slow down life*
> *if you want to speed it up for better days*
> *if you long for a family dinner together*
> *if you long for a moment to yourself*
> *if you want your kids to recognize the needs of others*
> *if you believe God has a purpose for your life*
> *if you want your life to count*
> *if you want what you do to matter*
>   *. . . this book is for you.*

Kristen Welch
JANUARY 2014

PROLOGUE

ARMED GUARDS WALKED ME, a group of other bloggers, and our guides down a muddy trail into Mathare Valley, one of Kenya's largest slums and most dangerous areas. We were observing and writing on behalf of Compassion International, who had arranged the trip.

I trembled from more than fear. There was hopelessness everywhere I looked—endless tiny tin shanties where hundreds of thousands of people were crowded, "homes" with no electricity or running water. Plastic bags full of sewage floated in a green stream, and the ground wasn't made of dirt at all—it was just a mountain of trampled garbage. The stench nearly gagged me.

A majority of the residents were small, unsupervised children. They called out to us, "How-ah-you? How-ah-you?" hoping we would put something into their upturned hands. We could see by their swollen bellies that they were malnourished. Their faces were filthy and covered with flies, which they didn't bother to shoo away.

It was a hellhole, not fit for the living.

I began to cry and couldn't stop. I wanted to shut it all out. I was angry with God. *Where are You? How can You allow so much suffering?*

Then I stopped and closed my eyes. I saw God's finger pointed at me as He asked my spirit the same question: *"Kristen, how can you allow this?"*

In that exact moment, I knew my life would never be the same.

I was a long way from home and my family. I was "just a mom." But my faith journey that started in high school had brought me to this point. Standing in this wretched place, I realized only He knew where it was going to lead.

CHAPTER 1

RHINESTONE JESUS

---✳︎---

People are like stained-glass windows. They sparkle and shine when the sun is out, but when the darkness sets in, their true beauty is revealed only if there is a light from within.

ELISABETH KÜBLER-ROSS

IT WAS MY FIRST DAY of tenth grade at Deer Park High School in Deer Park, Texas, and I sat in Algebra 2, the class right before lunch. But I wasn't thinking about equations. I was trying to figure out where I would sit in the cafeteria during lunch, a heavy question for most socially awkward introverts. I looked around the classroom. *I don't recognize anyone here!* My mind wandered back to my imminent dilemma. I could picture myself, tray in hand, searching the mass of students, looking for an empty spot. It was one of my recurring nightmares.

Just then I looked up and made eye contact with the girl sitting across from me in class. She smiled. It took more courage than I care to admit to whisper, "Where are you sitting at lunch?" I was glad to see a look of relief cross her face, and we made plans to sit together.

Meagan and I were an unlikely pair, but from that day on we shared a lunch table with a few other girls, all of us looking for a place to belong. I liked her, but I quickly learned we were very different.

I was an introverted good girl with a passion for thrift shopping, boys, and Jesus, not necessarily in that order. I lived in a Christian home, and church was a huge part of my life. I was *that* good girl: the one who carried her Bible to school and wore a rhinestone lapel pin that spelled out in sparkly letters J-E-S-U-S. (It was the late eighties, so it's not nearly as horrid as it sounds.)

It wasn't easy for me to talk about my faith; it was easier to let Rhinestone Jesus do the talking for me. Sure, there were days I wanted to fit in and be like everyone else, but I forced myself to pin it on because my desire to be known as a Christian kept me on the straight and narrow.

Between the Jesus pin, my Bible in my backpack, and my good-girl choices, I pretty much alienated myself from the popular kids. I was a different kind of nerd than the classic geek with taped glasses and a pocket protector, but I was a misfit nonetheless.

Still, in most ways I was a typical teen: I loved Friday night football games; hanging out with my twin sister, Kara, and friends at youth group events; and shopping. But my desire to act like a Christian made me completely atypical. It was uncommon for kids in my school to tuck their Bibles in their backpacks, lead the school Bible club, turn down dates with boys whom their parents didn't know, and have a closet full of T-shirts with Christian slogans or verses. I never missed youth group on Wednesday nights, and I always looked for opportunities to invite a friend to go with me.

After a couple of lunches, I learned Meagan was on the drill team and loved dancing, and although she wasn't quite as shy as I was, we had similar personalities. There was one big difference between us, though. She had quite the potty mouth.

A lot of kids in my school cussed, but I usually just ignored it. Still, I knew if Meagan and I were going to be true friends, I was going to have to speak up about it sooner or later. That day came pretty quickly. My cuss quota was at an all-time high, so I made one small decision that would ultimately alter my life in an unbelievable way. I rudely stopped Meagan midsentence and said in a rush, "I really want to be your friend, but do you think you could try not to cuss so much around me?"

Y'all, that was so hard to say!

"Why?" Meagan's question wasn't asked sarcastically or in a mean way. I took a deep breath and thought, *Because good girls don't cuss.* But what came out of my mouth was something uncharacteristically bold. "Because I'm a Christian and it makes me uncomfortable."

Meagan shrugged and said something like, "Okay. I'll try. I've never been to church."

From that moment, she made a conscious effort to clean up her language. But even better, Meagan started going to church with me. Before long, we were inseparable. I'll never forget the day, a couple of months later, when I led her to Christ on the right side of the sanctuary where the youth in our church sat. It was a Sunday night and she seemed fidgety and nervous, and so I came out with it: "Do you want to ask Jesus into your heart?" I remember hoping I was doing it right. I prayed a prayer and she repeated it. It was surreal, and it changed my life. All of the Sunday school classes and church services I'd attended since birth couldn't compare with the amazing experience of praying with someone to receive Jesus in her life for the first time.

Meagan became a student of the Bible. She kept me on my toes. She would call and ask me question after question: "What will heaven be like?" "Is hell real?" It was work to stay one step ahead of her. One day she called and said excitedly, "I've been reading the book of Job [she pronounced it like the synonym for *employment*], and that guy was amazing!" I distinctly remember I hadn't even opened my Bible that day. She was teaching me with her hunger for God. It didn't take long for me to realize that having a new believer follow in your footsteps was challenging, like nothing I had ever experienced before. It put to the test all the knowledge I'd received and stored in my head, and demanded action.

Somewhere between leading Meagan to Christ and witnessing her getting baptized in front of our church with her family attending, something deep and profound happened in my heart. I got it. Christianity wasn't about all the things I did for Jesus; it was about coming to know Him better and making disciples. Being a believer in Christ wasn't just an identity; it was a relationship.

I decided I wanted to change the world. I dreamed of lighting it on fire, doing something big and leaving my unique mark. I wasn't alone; there was a small group of us—my sister, Meagan, and a few others who also attended our church or school Bible club. Over the next two years, Meagan's faith continued to grow, and so did our friendship. (A few years later she came to my wedding, and ten years after high school we spent hours catching up at our class reunion. Today we are friends on Facebook and follow each other's lives closely.)

By my last year of high school, I was pegged as a hopelessly Christian girl. I lived by a long list of things I didn't do (cuss, drink, attend parties, have sex). But I also tried to be different from the world and the rest of my peers; I was the person many friends would turn to when they needed prayer. I still wore my pin most days. My theater arts program gave out silly "Napkin Awards" every year (awards printed on napkins). I received the "Rhinestone Jesus" award my senior year; it got a big laugh from the crowd, which stung a little. But for the most part, I was proud of my reputation.

Oh, and dates were rare. I can't blame the guys, really. I must have terrified them. I had my fair share of crushes on church boys and went out occasionally. Once I dated a darling boy from high school for three weeks. Luke was wildly popular and a terrible flirt. He invited me to the school Valentine's dance, so I invited him to church (missionary dating at its best). He came with me a few times (I can still remember his confusion as a Catholic boy visiting a Pentecostal church.) At the Valentine's dance, we danced one or two slow dances and ended up back at his empty house afterward. I'm still not sure if that was his plan, but I broke up with him a couple of days later, even though I liked him a lot. He was a nice boy who respected me, but I decided I wasn't the type to play with fire.

I was happy with who I was. I helped edit the school newspaper and discovered a deep love for writing. I owned an Apple Mac Classic, so clearly I was cool before my time. Writing quenched a natural hunger to express myself. I loved graphic design and using my new skills on the newspaper. I had an idea to create a T-shirt that featured a picture of the world turned upside down. The shirt would read, "I want to turn the world upside down for Jesus." I never made the shirt, but in my heart, it's exactly what I set out to do.

I would be lying if I didn't acknowledge that choosing this path made high school even harder than it already was. Exhausting. I was just a normal girl, and a part of me longed to fit in and be included. But in the end, I survived.

Meagan was the only person I led to Christ during high school. One girl. But I had put my faith into action and lived it out loud.

❋

When I was a junior thinking about college, my parents suggested two choices: San Jacinto College, which was a local community college, or Southwestern University in Waxahachie, Texas, a small private Bible college a few hours away. I applied to the Bible college, jumping at the chance for some freedom, which is funny, considering their strict 11 p.m. curfew and the demerits doled out for being closer than six inches to a boy. But I wanted to be in my element—a place where Rhinestone Jesus was expected to sparkle.

I loved attending a small Bible college. It was exactly what I had hoped it would be. But I was anxious to finish. So I attacked my studies like I did everything else: I overloaded my schedule with semester hours so I could finish my bachelor's degree in Christian education and my minor in English in three years and get on to world changing. I think that's called crazy.

On the second day of Bible college, I met a very interesting young man. I quickly noticed his tan, muscular legs on our intramural volleyball team and fell for his contagious personality. He was also one of the nicest people I'd ever met. Terrell was going to be a pastor, and that fit right into my plan. We ended up hanging out with the same circle of friends, playing cards and volleyball together. The college had a TWIRP (The Woman Is Required to Pay) Week, and I recycled an old deck of cards into an invitation and TWIRPed Terrell a few weeks after meeting him. I took him to a rowdy western restaurant, and he taught me how to two-step. Even though there were definitely sparks, he was a couple of years older than me and the timing felt wrong. A former girlfriend of Terrell's, who lived down the hall from me, started college the same week, and he realized he still had some unfinished feelings for her.

They started dating again, and she and I became dear friends, and Terrell and I began an amazing journey to becoming best friends. I dated one of Terrell's buddies, which turned out to be a painful on-and-off relationship. I would cry on Terrell's shoulder and he would share the disappointments of his relationship. After two years, we both ended up with broken hearts.

It took us four years to realize we were in love—and then suddenly, we were. (That's what happens when best friends kiss.) Terrell was in graduate school hours away from me, but our friendship grew only stronger over the years and miles. I graduated from college and my parents offered me a plane ticket to go on a trip. As I was telling Terrell over the phone one night about the gift, he invited me to come visit him at his parents' home, where he was working over the summer. That first night together, he kissed me on his parents' back porch, and I can still remember the fireworks. We got married ninety-eight days after that passionate first kiss.

So there we were—newlyweds, fresh-out-of-Bible-college newbies ready to start our lives together at a forty-year-old, troubled church in a small town in Arkansas. He was going

to be the youth pastor and I the children's pastor. We moved hundreds of miles from anyone we knew and right into the parsonage next to the church. We were armed and ready with plenty of Bible knowledge to turn the world upside down—or at least a town of twenty thousand.

Terrell's and my wedding day

And then life happened, and things didn't go as planned. Instead, the world slowly started sucking the dream right out of us. In the first few months of work, we learned the hard part of ministry was a lot like being pelted with popcorn. If someone throws a piece at you, it's irritating but basically harmless. But when they keep doing it until you're covered in popcorn, it can be hurtful and suffocating.

One Friday night, we fell into bed after a late-night youth event. The next thing we knew, someone was banging on our front door in the wee hours of Saturday morning, before the sun was up. In his haste, Terrell grabbed the first thing he found, pulled it on, and stumbled to the front door. There was a church member with his enormous RV parked in our driveway, demanding we open the church so he could fill up his ice chests with free ice from the church. My husband obliged, not realizing he was wearing my lace shirt.

Popcorn avalanche.

During our first year of marriage as youth and children's pastors, we discovered all the things we didn't learn in Bible college. Oh, you know—things like the fact that we would be poor and would need to work extra jobs like cleaning the church to pay our bills; and that people are mean, even Christians. I wasn't prepared for ministry to throw us into a glass house where everyone could see in and offer opinions on every area of our lives, from what I wore on Sundays and Mondays to having a pet in the parsonage. Our first job was a battlefield between a controlling board of elders and a heartbroken pastor, and as the new youth staffers, we were constantly caught in the middle.

We received a quick education in conflict, confrontation, and control. There were situations that left knots in our stomachs and ulcers in our mouths. We loved the kids we taught each week (and remain in touch with many of them to this day), and yet it was a very stressful, difficult beginning to our life together. We had some good days mixed in with the bad, but our first experience at "world changing" left us more broken than we could have dreamed. After two long-short years, we moved across the country to New Mexico to do it all over again in another church.

This time around, we expected the worst. I think that's just how we are as humans. We have high expectations about something or someone, and when we are disappointed, we adjust. In an attempt to protect ourselves, we put a guard around our hearts, and without realizing it, we began hardening them.

❋

In New Mexico we met people who would become lifelong friends, which turned out to be providential. Just as Terrell and I were discovering some fulfillment in ministry, we discovered the heartache of infertility in the midst of a church baby boom. I entered a dark season of depression.

Once our struggle got out (glass house, remember?), we were bombarded with advice from baby-makers. Everything was offered with good intentions as a way to support and encourage us; instead we felt embarrassed and isolated. I might have tried a couple of suggestions, but I drew the line at coffee enemas and standing on my head. I sank deeper into an emotional pit with every passing month.

It didn't take long for us to exhaust our financial resources. As church staff members, we didn't have infertility insurance coverage. We paid a couple of out-of-pocket expenses with the help of some family members, but when those options failed, we turned to adoption. I'd love to say we pursued adoption because of our desire to help a child in need, but in my fog of despair, I only saw my own need. Terrell and I endured a home study, completed mounds of paperwork, and answered hard questions on open adoption and teen birth mothers. Then we learned a girl we loved in our youth group was pregnant. She was keeping her baby.

This was a hard blow for me and nearly sent me over the edge. By that time, we'd been married five years. I ranted and raved and questioned God. *Why is life so difficult? I've been a good girl, a giving servant, a wannabe world-changer.* When life doesn't go according to our plans, we often turn on the divine Planner. In my pain, I couldn't see His hand. In my desperation, I didn't even know where to look for it.

I got to the place where I couldn't hold a friend's baby, and I would send gifts to baby showers rather than attend. I would hide in my church office during baby dedications and sob my way through Mother's Day. These were hard days for Terrell, too. While he felt the blow of each passing month, he mostly struggled to encourage me. He felt powerless. But in my pain, God was present. I didn't have answers, but I did have a friend who was experiencing the same pain of infertility. God used Robin to remind me I wasn't alone.

We finally got a call from an interested birth mother, and to make a long story short, she wanted her baby to go to a childless couple and asked if I would take a pregnancy test. Of course— no problem! I had peed on more sticks than I could count in my quest for a baby, so I knew the drill.

And that's when I discovered I was pregnant with our first child. I simply couldn't believe that after so many years of struggle, we were pregnant when we least expected it. I sent my husband to the store to buy more pregnancy tests, and we tried to absorb the amazing news. We were both shocked. I was terrified I would have a miscarriage, but with every passing day, the tiny baby in me grew and so did my peace.

At one point, after I'd endured a queasy morning and tossed my breakfast in the master bathroom, I whined to my husband about my constant nausea. Terrell started laughing. "Yes! This is exactly what we wanted. This is pregnancy!"

I sort of wanted to punch him at that moment. But I had to laugh too. He was exactly right.

Terrell and I rejoiced in new life while we mourned an adoption that wasn't to be. It was a roller-coaster season of fear and relief, but it was also an exciting new chapter. I was beginning to realize that hardships in life shape us, struggles define us, and both ultimately prepare us for the future God is calling us to.

My dream to change the world hadn't disappeared, but it had definitely been tarnished—a lot like the old rhinestone pin that occupied a corner of my jewelry box. God was trying to teach me to put my trust in Him.

I turned out to be a stubborn student.

❁ ❀ ❁

UNPINNED FAITH

You may not be as stubborn as I am, but I think most of us view roadblocks in our path of life as setbacks. These obstacles alter our journeys and often leave us discouraged. But God provides detours if we pay attention. When we choose to see His alternate route as an opportunity for something new rather than a dead end, it shifts our perspective.

With that in mind, take a few moments to reflect right now. Think back to your younger days. Did you have childhood dreams? Even in our childhood wishes, we can often discover what our hearts were like before they were hardened by the harsh reality of life. What events in your life have quieted or completely quenched your dreams? Did reality turn your dare into despair? When I'm feeling this way, I like to encourage myself that my life isn't over and God has a plan. In Philippians 1:6, the apostle Paul says, "Being confident of this, that he who began a good work in you will carry it on to completion until the day of Christ Jesus."

I hope that if you've maneuvered through God's detour, you can look back and see how that difficulty has changed you for the better. And don't stop dreaming.

Are there dreams you still long to pursue? Write them down. And don't give up.

————— ❁ —————

CHAPTER 2

WHEN MOTHERHOOD BECOMES YOU

❋

Before you were conceived I wanted you.
Before you were born I loved you. Before you were a minute old
I would have died for you. This is the miracle of life.

MAUREEN HAWKINS

WHEN I WAS TWELVE years old, my parents took my siblings and me to have family pictures taken at the Sears Portrait Studio. It was a big deal because treats like this were rare. I wore a mauve sweater with tiny embroidered bears and my best blue jeans; clearly, *I had it going on.*

A few years ago, my mom gave me a box of old photographs, and I found that family portrait toward the bottom of the pile. Two things stood out in the photo and made my kids laugh hysterically when they saw it: one, I had enormous permed hair (my mom sort of had a gift for home hair care), and two, I was holding a lifelike baby doll on my lap. Awkward.

I remember that as I was getting ready that day, my mom said we could bring a favorite toy with us for the portraits. My sister brought her Cabbage Patch doll, and I'm pretty sure my older brother just rolled his eyes. I still played with dolls. Obviously. The 1980s doll I was pictured with was one of the first battery-powered, lifelike babies that sucked a pacifier. I used to pretend she was real and that someone had dropped her off on our back porch in a basket. I had discovered her there and decided to raise her as my own.

See? Had it. Going *on*.

But something happened between my twelfth and thirteenth years. I stopped playing with my baby doll and started playing sports. I replaced doll clothes and imagination with a basketball and my first crush on a boy. I suddenly longed to burn that family picture hanging on the living room wall with me hanging on to my doll. Most girls my age had started babysitting and working in the church nursery. I didn't. I don't really know why. I must have exhausted all my nurturing on dolls.

I never really thought about motherhood or babies again until I was nearly married. Terrell and I visited his family for the holidays, and his two infant nephews were there. I was slightly uncomfortable around them and silently hoped nobody needed a diaper change on my watch. Terrell was the exact opposite. I remember watching in awe as the man I was going to marry handled babies like a pro. He was a natural, and it made me feel better knowing that if we ever had kids, he'd know what to do.

Years later, when I was a children's pastor and a wife, my life centered around kids. I loved the way they saw God, and I loved teaching them about Him. I spent my days preparing for vacation Bible schools and leading kids' services, and somewhere between nieces and nephews and church work, I started wanting a child of my own.

Now that I was pregnant, I absorbed every book on the subject. Terrell and I sat through birthing classes, and he followed me as I waddled my way down the baby aisle, registering for items I would never use. Our first baby was ten days overdue, and after years of infertility, I was more than ready to be a mother.

But the minute Madison (our "miracle," which is also one of the meanings of her name) came screaming defiantly into the world, I knew I wasn't really ready to be a mother at all. My mother marveled at my tiny one's strong will as she raised her head off the table just minutes after being born and looked around the room, yelling to announce herself. I believe that's what you call foreshadowing.

I fell deeply in love with my baby girl and instantly entered the world of mothers, where talking about breast milk and constipation was not only accepted, it was appreciated. But Madison cried a lot, rarely slept, and seemed content only when I was holding her. Terrell had to return to work soon after she was born so we were both glad my parents were visiting to help me adjust. One day, as my mom changed her granddaughter's tiny socks, Madison screamed like she was dying. My mom snuggled her close and said, "She's a demanding little thing."

I bristled. *My perfect baby was demanding?* My mom didn't mean anything negative by her comment; she knew how challenging babies could be. It didn't take long for me to find out just what she was talking about. It's the simple concept of supply and demand: from birth on, children are created to be needy. And from mother's milk to a mother's heart, we meet their needs. It's a partnership like no other, created by the hand of God. It's breathtaking, and some days, it takes your breath away trying to keep up.

Three months into motherhood, I sat terrified across from a tiny human who had become the boss of me. My energy supply was running a bit low and her demand was high. My husband worked long hours and my parents lived far away. It was just the two of us. Madison and I fell into a new routine, but I felt alone. I lost my identity, my freedom, and ultimately, control.

Some women embrace motherhood. Others are embraced by motherhood. But either way, it changes all of us in ways we never expected.

I smelled like spit-up and struggled with self-image. I went from being a working woman to a working mother, with heavy emphasis on *working*. My neat little house suddenly wasn't, laundry took on a life of its own (what is it with baby bodily fluids and soft cotton?), my body became a food source, and worry became my middle name. *What does that cry mean? What if she reacts to her vaccines? What if I am a horrible mother?* My entire life came down to one insistent little girl who wanted most of my time and energy.

I wasn't ready to be lost to motherhood, *for it to become me.* But it did, and I wasn't sure how I felt about being lost on a journey of my own choosing. Madison grew older, and although I continued on a part-time basis at the church, working mostly from home, I tried to understand my new identity. With each passing day, I fell deeper into mothering, lost a little more of myself, and watched my dream of changing the world fade.

Losing myself to motherhood was good in many ways. From the moment of conception and the onset of nausea and vomiting, mothering taught me to be selfless. It became natural to put my child's needs in front of my own. Even in bewildering exhaustion, I stumbled through midnight feedings and all the ups and downs of motherhood because it's what we do.

But even in selflessness, we find the root word, *self*. As I intuitively sacrificed for my child, the need to take care of myself magnified. I saw how much my helpless baby depended on me, and it intensified my desire to be present and become someone she would want to emulate. Easier said than done.

✳

In my first few years of adjusting to my new role, I made a lot of mistakes. (And I'm not referring to buying a "colic machine" that vibrated my crying baby's crib. Scam. I got a refund.) I worried a lot and second-guessed myself. *Why is she crying? Is she hungry? Why won't she sleep?* I struggled with trying to control this new little human. Some days I spent hours trying to get my baby to sleep, and other days I would go to great lengths to wake my sleeping baby so I could feed her. I think one of my biggest mistakes was not taking enough time for myself. I probably would have blamed it on being financially strapped, but it was also simple neglect.

Baby Madison and me

My glaring inadequacies were more noticeable, and I began to understand for the first time as a new parent how God feels about me, His child. Parenting is God's mirror: it shows us a reflection of ourselves as we really are. I see myself in my children—good traits and bad—the way God sees me. If you've ever had a two-year-old have a complete meltdown, kicking and screaming included, in a quiet library filled with serious book readers, you know what I mean. I'll never forget marching my child back in the next day so we could apologize, hoping the librarians wouldn't recognize us from the noisy scene the day before. They knew exactly who we were. I don't think I went back to the library for a year after that episode.

I am stubborn too. I want freedom and choices. I want things my way. God is always there, a constant. He never stops loving me. He is patient. He waits. I can see it now: the reflection. The gentle way He parents me. His discipline comes from abiding love. "Yes, I'm beginning to understand, God." Thankfully, God isn't repelled by our neediness.

Mothering is a journey. We don't ever truly arrive. As our children grow, their needs change. Problems come and go, but they will always be our kids. I still call my mom when I need her, and she still comes. I don't want to wish away today, thinking tomorrow will be easier with my children. I want to live today the best I can and learn from it. Mothering is more about me growing up than my children. I used to think becoming a parent meant I knew something, but the longer I'm a mom, the more I realize how much I don't know.

One day I was talking on the phone to Betty, my sweet mother-in-law. My kids had just returned from a week at their grandparents' farm, and I was getting the details of their visit. I asked Betty if Jon-Avery (eleven years old at the time) had gotten along with his sisters while we were away. He is a natural peacemaker—his naturally bossy big and little sisters have been telling me what to do for years.

"Oh, he was fine," Betty said. "He was a big help around the farm, and they got along pretty well. But, oh, is that boy noisy!" I started laughing because I had noticed he had started a phase where he was constantly making noises and sounds with his mouth or tapping and drumming on things with his fingers.

And then Betty enlightened me. "Oh, Kristen, I hate to tell you, but this phase lasts *for years*." Well, I did not know that. Just when we get through one stage, another begins.

Parenting is physical when our kids are little. Babies and toddlers command exhausting, hands-on help. Parenting becomes less physical and more emotional as our children grow up. People who love each other sometimes hurt each other. Words are blurted out that shouldn't have been said, and suddenly we find out if our lessons about forgiveness really stuck. In just a matter of time, we go from trying to get our babies to say our name to hiding in the bathroom when they won't quit saying it over and over.

My youngest child told me the other day that she wanted to be president of the United States.

"Really?" I asked. "Because you want to change the world?"

"No," she answered. "I just really want to be the boss of you."

Mothering is the hardest thing I've ever done and also the best. It's the most demanding, challenging area in my life. At the same time, growing these little people is the most fulfilling, meaningful work I've ever done. It's full of ups and downs. But I'm determined to love them well. God uses my kids to teach me about myself every day. Ultimately, He shows me that I can't be the mom I long to be on my own. I need His help.

❀

By the time I felt like I was finally adjusting to becoming a mother, I found out I was pregnant with my second child. Surprise! I was cautiously excited (which is another way of saying I cried because my hands were already full with an on-the-go eighteen-month-old). At the same time, I honestly wondered whether I would ever do anything "big" for God.

"Smashing bananas and wiping chins, googling homemade diaper rash remedies, and childproofing cabinets don't feel like changing the world, God." I knew these things were necessary, but they all felt small and unimportant. Many days my life seemed mundane and messy. I'll admit that when your baby has a fever and you are feverish for something more, it's hard to find God under the laundry pile. And then a still, small voice says, "When you serve the least of these, you are serving Me." Okay, You got me.

The Kingdom of God is revealed in sacrifice and service in the small places, especially to our children. It probably won't make the evening news or maybe even be noticed by our spouses unless we tell them, but in a quiet, obscure place, we are changing the world. Because here's the truth we must believe: we might not be able to change the *whole* world, but as moms we can change *one* person's world. And there is power in one.

I saw a glimpse of this a few months ago in the park. I was chatting with a lady I didn't know as I watched my youngest and her child play on the swings.

We were barely getting acquainted when she asked, "Do you know what kids really want from their moms?"

"Cell phones," I said, laughing and thinking of my oldest, who was now a teen.

The other mother smiled, but her eyes were tearing up. "We spend a lot of time trying to figure out what our kids want and need in this life." How true. I often try to figure out what's really wrong with my kids. When they were babies, I spent countless hours and gobs of energy trying to discern hunger from exhaustion. Now that they are older, there is a new set of endless questions: *How do I help them choose the best friends? She is hurting; what can I do? How do I help instill confidence in him?*

"It's pretty simple," the woman said. "Your kids want you."

Boom.

"When they say, 'Mom, watch me,' they just want you. When they pull you away from whatever you are doing, it's because they want you." And then she got up and left.

I sat there, both convicted and freed by her words. They jolted my heart awake. My kids don't need me to fix their problems. They don't need me to provide more stuff or help them try to keep up with everyone else. I thought back to the times when I was asked to "take a look at this," and I was too busy to stop what I was doing. I vowed from that day forward to be present in the moment as much as I possibly could.

"God, I realize they need me, but even more, they need You. I need You because this mothering thing is awesome and hard. When I look back, I won't remember the days. I will remember the moments. And I'm thankful for that because, believe me, there are days I don't want to remember!"

I do want to remember the drive on the way to school this morning. The way my daughter laughed. The moment she opened up and shared her thoughts. The way our hearts connected. Those treasured moments make up for the rest of the day with the exaggerated eye rolls and exasperated sighs. It's all part of this job.

Instead of asking myself, *Is her room clean? Did he ace that test?* I'm asking, *Did I connect with them in a way that I will remember twenty years from now? Did I listen when she called my name four times? Did our hearts meet for a brief moment? Did he know that even when I couldn't fix the problem, I was there for him?*

At my house, rooms are still messy, floors are still sticky, and laundry still piles up. After all these years as a mother, I've accepted the fact that there will be good and bad days. I lose my cool, pick my battles, and say a lot of I'm sorrys. But in a few years, when my house is quiet and my children are gone, I will be able to recall the precious minutes when I stopped everything and just loved them because that's what God wants me to do.

Looking at my life, some people would say I have gotten to do some big things for God. But the most significant thing I've done for Jesus is to love and serve my family. Motherhood becomes me, and God uses it daily to refine me and draw me closer to Him.

UNPINNED FAITH

If you're a mom (or hope to be one someday), you most likely struggle with a bit of mom guilt every now and then. It creeps in when we don't live up to the image of the mom we think we should be. It's always been a struggle for me, and I learned a long time ago that I am one of my own worst enemies. God has been teaching me to change my focus. Instead of viewing life through a giant lens and giving myself an overall grade for the day, month, or year (we tend to be harder on ourselves than on anyone else), I focus on one goal: to connect with my children every day in some small way. Because let's face it, kids won't remember half the things we tell them are important, but they will remember when we shared a cup of hot chocolate together or painted each other's fingernails. Love is never wasted. "Love bears all things, believes all things, hopes all things, endures all things. Love never ends" (1 Corinthians 13:7-8, ESV).

That doesn't mean you should neglect yourself. Wherever you are in your mothering journey, you have to add yourself to the priority list. What have you done for yourself lately? With the demands of mothering, it's easy to fall into the trap of meeting everyone else's needs and ignoring your own. Make a list of some things you'd like to do for yourself. Here are some ideas:

- Enroll in a class
- Get an annual checkup
- Schedule a massage or pedicure
- Buy yourself a new pair of jeans
- Make your own favorite meal
- Pursue a hobby
- Have coffee with a girlfriend

CHAPTER 3

FINDING BEAUTY
IN THE BROKEN PIECES

❋

God uses broken things. It takes broken soil to produce a crop,
broken clouds to give rain, broken grain to give bread,
broken bread to give strength.
It is the broken alabaster box that gives forth perfume. . . .
It is Peter, weeping bitterly, who returns to greater power than ever.

VANCE HAVNER

I STOOD IN THE KITCHEN of our little home and stirred soup. By this time, we had moved to our third and final church job in Florida. We were thousands of miles from home with a new-born son and a willful two-year-old. Moving across the country, pregnant with adventure and our second child, had seemed like a great idea a few months before. But reality ended up being a home that was in disrepair, a high cost of living that cost us more than we had, a new life without friends or family in a strange city, and a new job Terrell hated. He worked for a church leader who wasn't pleased with anything he did. I found a part-time job tutoring to help make ends meet, but it forced me to wean my newborn much sooner than I was planning, which contributed to a horrible case of postpartum depression. I was miserable. My husband was miserable. Our home was miserable. Looking back, I think we were running from discontentment and ingratitude. And we ran right into a situation that made us wish for what we had previously complained about.

After I ladled chowder into the bowls, I carried my beautiful porcelain pitcher full of sweet tea to the table. Without warning, the brightly colored pitcher slipped from my hand. I watched it fall in slow motion and shatter on the floor. Colorful shards bounced and scattered, broken pieces of a once-useful vessel. The floor was covered with bright red and yellow ceramic chunks and jagged turquoise triangles.

I leaned over and carefully scooped up the larger pieces, angry at my carelessness, before I swept up the remaining fragments. As I sopped up sticky tea with paper towels, I was sad at the loss of my pretty pitcher. I wasn't ready to part with it—even though I knew I couldn't make it whole again. I decided to wash off the shards and store them in a plastic container, thinking, *Maybe I can create something from the pieces later.*

As I cleaned up the mess, I pondered the strength of pottery, created for service. Or was it really weakness, fashioned for fracturing? Either way, it was no match for an unsteady hand and an unforgiving tile floor. In the months to come, I would learn about the weakness and strength of our little family. We would falter and fail and taste brokenness like we couldn't imagine. My solid marriage would be unrecognizable, a lot like the pieces scattered around me.

Our "ground zero" moment occurred just months after we left full-time ministry.

In the months leading up to it, I carried heavy sadness with me, the kind of sorrow that comes when you stop dreaming.

Curled up next to Terrell one night, I thought about staying in bed forever.

I'll never forget what he said to me: "What happened to the girl I married? The one who was going to change the world?"

My words hammered in my chest. "I don't even dream of changing the world anymore. I just want to survive it."

His response filled our bedroom. "We used to be dreamers. *What happened to us?*"

Life happened.

I spent my days wishing for better ones. We had bills piling up from a broken-down house and a growing family on a church income. Terrell was leaving at the crack of dawn every morning for the church, to be back in time so I could make it to my part-time tutoring job. Tag-team parenting our infant son and two-year-old daughter, we were caught up in the hectic rat race of life. It seemed we were constantly running and bogged down in things that didn't really matter, while time slipped through our fingers. I fantasized about the future and was losing the beauty of every day.

The night Terrell asked the question was a turning point. My quick response terrified him. "What if we quit? Let's just resign and move back home. We don't belong here."

We whispered words long into the night, coupled with tangible fear and tears: "What will we do?" "How will we live?" "Are we really brave enough to do something different?" When we finally were courageous enough to speak of our desperation, we knew we had to make a choice. We were tired of just surviving and being miserable; we wanted to live again. We sought the counsel of our supportive family and were relieved they didn't think we were crazy.

My husband resigned from the church the very next day, I quit my tutoring job, and we sold our house in a week. It was just the encouragement we needed to take the biggest risk of our lives (so far).

We loaded up our lives and moved back to Texas, closer to family. It was a scary time. With just the (very) small equity from our town house in our pocket, we started over in a small town house my dad owned. We paid him a reduced rent from our equity. It took my husband six long and wonderful months to find a job (amazingly, the same one he still has today, going on ten years). Although those six months were uncertain as we watched our savings account slowly drain, they were also like taking a long, deep breath. For the first time in our marriage, we were on the other side of the pulpit. We could skip church if we wanted to—but we rarely did because we'd found a great church that had a small ministry to former pastors, where we realized we weren't the only ones hurt by ministry. Terrell did some consulting work for my dad's business while he looked for a full-time job.

Ironically, I got a part-time job in the children's ministry of our new church. It was refreshing to be a part of a healthy church body. We had always lived very frugally, and this season was no different. And while it was challenging, we loved being near my family. My sister lived down the street from us, and my parents were only a couple of miles away. For the first time, my kids had cousins and grandparents as part of their everyday lives. We were still desperate. Desperate to start living again and figure out the next steps without letting our lives run us. But we have never once regretted stepping away from what was safe and known.

The first decade of our marriage had been spent under the

scrutiny that often comes with full-time ministry. We were constantly watched and questioned by people. It's tricky territory and a sad commentary on pastoral life. I remember being berated once for getting my ears pierced with a second earring. The mom was angry because "now her daughter would want to do the same thing." It didn't seem to occur to her that I was nearly thirty years old and her daughter was twelve. Nevertheless, we have some beautiful memories of our time working in churches. These experiences were preparing us for the God-sized dream He would reveal later, but we both knew this season was ending.

It was during that period of concentrated time together that our glass house shattered. For the first time in our married lives, we felt like we could breathe freely. It was a period where we struggled with our identity and roles and, mostly, our calling. We had always wanted to be in full-time ministry and had never just "attended" church as a family. This change brought everything out in the open, and we talked and prayed and cried a lot. And learned deep things about each other, even though we thought we knew it all.

❋

"I need to tell you something."

It was my twenty-third birthday, two days after our one-year wedding anniversary in 1996. Terrell and I were on an overnight getaway to hear a popular evangelist we both admired. We were out on a date after the service and had just celebrated my birthday dinner at a restaurant. We got back in the car to head to the hotel, and with the taste of birthday cake still fresh in my mouth, I heard my brand-new husband tell me he had found a tattered *Playboy* magazine in a trash pile when he was collecting barn wood for a children's-church puppet stage he was building a couple of weeks before.

I stared at him blankly.

"I stopped working, pulled off my work gloves, and looked through it."

I'll never forget the look of guilt and remorse on his face or the bitter taste in my mouth.

"It's my birthday and you've ruined it," I said like a spoiled little girl. And then I started a horrible, crying tantrum filled with threats and insults and all the wrong things. *Of course. We just left church and something the evangelist said tonight must have made Terrell feel guilty, and that's why he decided to come clean. He just needed to get it off his chest. But why on my birthday? Nice present.*

I never thought my young husband was attempting to let me know about a private struggle. I did what he feared most: I made him feel worse because my good-girl mentality was horrified that my good boy had made such a terrible choice. My reaction warned him to never speak of it again.

I was extremely naive and completely clueless about men and the way they think. The two of us had been able to suppress natural sexual desires when we were in Bible school, keeping our commitment to marry as virgins. Not that it was easy. So when Terrell admitted this to me, I was surprised and disappointed and totally bewildered as to *why* there had been this temporary lapse of character. But I was afraid to process it and didn't like the way his choice made me feel as a woman, so I pretended everything was okay. Terrell did the same. What's worse, I didn't even know we were pretending.

I squelched the one question I knew I should have asked: "Why did you look?" Looking back, I realize it would have opened the door to a problem I didn't know existed because I had convinced myself it didn't.

After some pouting and getting assurance from him, I acted like the one-time breach of trust had never occurred. Much to my relief, he never mentioned the word *pornography* again.

We survived the early poor years, overcame infertility and became parents, encountered difficult ministry positions, rejoiced at the depth that comes from stability, and still maintained a fairly ideal marriage through it all. With every trial and victory, our friendship deepened.

Then we got access to the Internet.

※

It was 2005, and we were weeks away from celebrating ten years of marriage. Now that Terrell was working full time at his sales job, we decided to take a long-overdue family vacation to Disney World—our first real time away since leaving ministry. We had saved and planned for over six months, getting as much information as we could ahead of time to make this a *fairy-tale* week for us and our two kids. It turned out to be just that.

We were on the long drive home from Florida to Texas, with the kids asleep in the back of our van, still wearing their mouse ears. I was tired, too, but on an emotional high that came from making their dreams come true.

I was talking to Terrell, trying to help him stay awake on the road. The conversation was light; we laughed and enjoyed each other's company. We were just talking, and then I remembered I wanted to ask him if we could give an offering from his recent bonus to Ty and his wife, dear friends of ours who were struggling in full-time ministry. As soon as the words came out, my husband's mood darkened. His tone changed and the atmosphere in the van grew tense.

"What's wrong?" I asked innocently.

"Ty hasn't been a very good friend to me. He has really let me down," he said curtly.

I had no idea what he was referring to, and I pressed for more information. Since we were living in different states, I couldn't imagine what our good friend had done. That's when Terrell told me Ty had struggled with pornography. As we talked about his friend's poor choices, Terrell was being torn apart inside. I still didn't understand why he wouldn't want to forgive and bless our friend.

What I didn't know in that moment was that a couple of years earlier, Terrell had confided his ongoing struggle with pornography to Ty over the phone. His friend promised to walk with him to freedom. Only he never did. My husband didn't hear from Ty until a couple of weeks before our trip to Disney World. He was calling to confess his own long-term struggle and ask for forgiveness. It turned out pornography was his own secret sin.

"What are you saying?" I asked slowly, methodically, in a fog of denial.

Terrell couldn't go another second, say another word, without revealing his own secret sin.

"I'm angry because when I needed his help, he let me down. I need help. I have the same problem."

What did he just say?

My heart splintered into a thousand pieces. It was like an out-of-body experience, surreal. *This can't be real. I must have misunderstood him. He's telling me about his friend; this isn't my husband's secret.*

But it was: my husband had just told me he was addicted to pornography. Just like that, the fairy tale ended.

✳

I unbuckled my seat belt and climbed into the back of our van where my children were sleeping. I had to get away from this stranger. I crouched between their two car seats, pulled my knees up to my chin, and cried. I stayed back there for a long time until I could finally make eye contact with the person in the rearview mirror I had thought I knew.

In the shadows, I could see Terrell's shoulders shaking and the tears streaming down his face. I was watching a man break in two. He sobbed with relief, the kind that comes from unleashing pent-up pain hidden for far too long. I was horrified at his confession, disgusted and confused. At the same time, I longed to wipe his cheeks and cling to him. He kept saying, "I'm sorry, I'm so sorry, I had to tell you." He paused. Then, "Even if it means you can't stay married to me. I can't live like this any longer."

As I huddled in the back of the van, I wanted a distraction. I wanted to wake my sleeping children. I wanted them to need me. I wanted to pretend a little bit longer. But they slept on while the man in the front seat begged me to say something. I racked my brain searching for clues to what had led us to this moment. I couldn't reconcile the man I loved with the man he had just confessed to be. I loved my best friend and partner, but I didn't know this side of him, and it scared me to death.

My hands shook and I struggled to breathe. Tears splashed on my babies, and I wanted to die. I hated Terrell for his confession, for the years of lies he must have told, and for being someone I had thought he couldn't be. He had unloaded the burden of his life on me, and now I carried the damage of it. I didn't understand the entrapments of his sin, why he couldn't find freedom, and what role I played in all of it. Even the thought of beginning this journey turned my stomach.

But simultaneously, I loved him for telling me. I ached at his desperation, and I couldn't comprehend what this confession had cost him, knowing what the consequences might be. I couldn't imagine my life without this guy. I didn't want to live without him, I didn't want him absent from our kids' lives, but I couldn't even fathom tomorrow. *What do we do now? Will he ever be free? How will I ever forgive him? When will I wake up from this hell?*

And so I offered the only words I could think of: "We can live as friends."

Immediately, I saw momentary relief in his eyes. But the rear-view mirror also revealed a depth of sadness in my husband that shook me. He saw raw fear and pain in my eyes. We couldn't bear it, and we both looked away. With hours of driving left, I climbed back to my seat, and we began the conversation that would break my heart even more when I dared to ask *why.*

Because no matter how he answered that question, I didn't know the man I was married to, and I began to wonder if his struggle was my fault.

The escape and perfection I had found at Disney World suddenly seemed so far away and even silly. I thought over our week of memories, of laughter and happiness, and wondered if it was all make-believe just like the pretend world we had visited. This was the beginning of a long and gut-wrenching quest for freedom and forgiveness.

But something miraculous happened in the midst of our devastation. The very night Terrell took a bold step and confessed his struggle to me was the same night I stepped toward him and started the process of forgiveness. Everything in me wanted to run away from this stranger I loved. But at the same time, I was so proud of him for wanting freedom more than he wanted to continue in the safety of his secret. We sobbed our way through intimacy that night, and even though we had never tasted so much brokenness, we knew that somehow God would redeem the ashes. We knew it would be the greatest battle of our lives—this choice to walk in freedom and forgiveness—but we decided in the middle of our devastation that we would fight for wholeness in our marriage.

✳

In the days after, I mourned the loss of my innocence and the marriage I'd thought I had. I was angry and felt like my world was spiraling out of control. Forgiveness is often a hard daily choice, and sometimes the pain of the situation was stronger than my desire to forgive. I couldn't eat or sleep and thought too much while I was awake. We didn't confide in anyone in the beginning. It was too hard to say the words out loud, and we were ashamed. Terrell and I knew we needed help. He started reading *Every Man's Battle* by Stephen Arterburn and Fred Stoeker, and I read *I Surrender All: Rebuilding a Marriage Broken by Pornography* by Clay and Renee Crosse. While these books helped us realize we weren't alone, we were desperate for more resources and tools, so we began marriage counseling just a week after returning home.

I'll never forget dropping our two preschool-age children off at my parents' house unannounced. I knew they could tell something was wrong because I was trying not to cry. "Mom,

I just need you to take them for a while. Don't ask why. Terrell and I need to work on our marriage." And my amazing parents watched our children without pressing us as we shared our brokenness with a godly counselor for weeks.

My life was fractured, and I tasted brokenness with every passing moment. Even though Terrell and I were taking steps toward healing, I realized my own mind was a battlefield. I wanted all the gory details from my husband—the what, when, and how of his fight with pornography. But it didn't take long to realize I didn't need to know them.

During a couple of our first counseling sessions, I was confused as to why Bob, our counselor, kept turning his attention to me. I kept thinking, *My husband has the problem. Help him! Please!* When I mentioned this to Bob, he explained to me how light Terrell's addiction was.

"Kristen, your husband has barely scratched the surface of this dark world. He has never given into it completely. He has fought a long and hard battle, and I am proud of him. I have no doubt he will overcome this struggle because he wants to and he's seeking God for help. I will give him a few tools, but you're the one I'm concerned about."

I had fallen into a deep cycle—I was not only blaming myself for Terrell's struggle, I was also feeling inadequate as a wife and a woman. While my husband was feeling more free with each passing day, I was feeling more burdened with his confession. Bob began to minister to me and remind me of who I was in Jesus. I was enough because Christ in me was enough.

I had another turning point as I read *For Women Only* by Shaunti Feldhahn. In her book, Shaunti describes how men think and who they are at their core. I realized through counseling and by reading this enlightening book how very naive I was concerning men—how they think, how visual they are, how often they physically need sex. I was beginning to understand how God created my husband, and I was learning who I was in the process.

In my grief, I clung to God—not because I was spiritual, but because I saw my desperate need for Him. Terrell and I were praying and reading the Bible together with a fervency we had never known. I trusted God with my broken heart, and He slowly began to put the pieces of my life back together. What Rick Warren said was true: "Your most profound and intimate experiences of worship will likely be in your darkest days—when your heart is broken, when you feel abandoned, when you're out of options, when the pain is great—and you turn to God."[1]

❋

It took a long year of counseling and hard, late-into-the-night talks for us to come to the point of being able to look back and actually thank God for this broken place. We armed ourselves with tools to combat our minds, which were our most powerful enemies. We took a thousand small steps to gain trust again. We had setbacks along the way in our progress to restoration. I realized that just as I have weaknesses with wanting control, losing my temper, and speaking before I think sometimes, one of my husband's weaknesses is lust. It was hard for me to accept that because it feels more damaging than my sins. But God would remind me in those moments of doubt and fear that being tempted isn't being sinful. God had given my husband self-control over his temptation, and he walked in freedom from the bondage of his weakness. Above all, God brought grace into our home. Grace to be human and love each other when we were weak.

Terrell and I made our marriage a top priority in our busy lives. He even turned down a promotion that would take him away from home more often. After we stopped counseling, we continued to fall deeper in love by making God more a part of our daily marriage—asking hard questions, praying together, encouraging each other, going on romantic dates, and sending one another notes.

Terrell explains what was going on inside of him.

One of the most remarkable things happened in the middle of this mess that I had made. I watched my wife do something beyond comprehension. She loved me. She held me. She offered forgiveness. Every natural reaction of disgust, hatred, and loathing was replaced by an opposite and more powerful action of acceptance, love, and compassion. She put everything she had into my recovery and fought for our marriage like a cornered dog.

As this process unfolded, I came to realize that while I "knew" God loved me and would forgive me, I didn't really believe it. In spite of my doubts, Kristen continued to model unconditional love and forgiveness. Somewhere in the middle of our disaster, I was overwhelmed with a deep and real sense of God's love for me. When Kristen asked me later, "What made the difference?" I told her, "You did. You became Jesus with skin on and showed me what His love was really like."

I've never again doubted God's love for me, because I saw it. I lived it. I felt it. I experienced it.

Kristen asked me one day to sum up what I felt about the journey of forgiveness that we had been on. I recounted the story to her that I had used many times as a youth pastor.

In the 1800s, a young Englishman traveled to California in search of gold. He struck it rich after several months of prospecting. On his way home, he stopped in New Orleans. While there, he came upon a crowd of people [all] looking in the same direction. It didn't take long to see why the crowd had gathered. The people had gathered for a slave auction. He heard "Sold!" just as he joined the crowd. A middle-aged black man was taken away.

A beautiful young black girl was then pushed onto the platform and made to walk around so everyone could see her. The miner heard vile jokes and comments that spoke of evil intentions from those around him. Men were laughing as their eyes remained fixed on this new item for sale.

The bidding began.

Within a minute, the bids surpassed what most slave owners would pay. . . . As the bidding continued higher and higher, it was apparent that two men wanted her. In between their bids, they laughed about what they were going to do with her, and how the other one would miss out. The miner stood silent as anger welled up inside him. One man finally bid a price that was beyond the reach of the other. The girl looked down. The auctioneer called out, "Going once! Going twice!"

Just before the final call, the miner yelled out a price that was exactly twice the previous bid. This amount exceeded the worth of any man. The crowd laughed, thinking that the miner was only joking. The auctioneer motioned to the miner to come and show his money. The miner opened his bag of gold. The auctioneer shook his head in disbelief as he waved the girl over to him.

The girl walked down the steps of the platform until she was eye-to-eye with the miner. She spat straight in his face and said through clenched teeth, "I hate you!" The miner, without a word, wiped his face, paid the auctioneer, took the girl by the hand, and walked away from the still laughing crowd.

He seemed to be looking for something in particular as they walked up one street and down another. He finally stopped in front of a store, though the slave girl did not know what type of store it was. She waited outside as the dirty-faced miner went inside and started talking to an elderly man. She couldn't make out what they were talking about. At one point, the voices got louder and she overheard the store clerk say, "But it's the law! It's the law!" Peering in she saw the miner pull out his bag of gold and pour what was left on the table.

With what seemed like a look of disgust, the clerk picked up the gold and went into a back room. He came out with a piece of paper that both he and the miner signed.

The young girl looked away as the miner came out the door. Stretching out his hand he said to the girl, "Here are your manumission papers. You are free." The girl did not look up.

He tried again. "Here. These are papers that say you are free. Take them."

"I hate you!" the girl said, refusing to look up. "Why do you make fun of me?"

"No, listen," he pleaded. "These are your freedom papers. You are a free person."

The girl looked at the papers, then looked at him, and looked at the papers once again. "You just bought me . . . and now, you're setting me free?"

"That's why I bought you. I bought you to set you free."

The beautiful young girl fell to her knees in front of the miner, tears streaming down her face. "You bought me to set me free! You bought me to set me free!" she said over and over. The miner said nothing.

Clutching his muddy boots, the girl looked up at the miner and said, "All I want to do is serve you—because you bought me to set me free."[2]

"How do I feel about this journey of forgiveness that we've been on?" Terrell repeated the question back to me. "I feel like the slave girl at that auction."

Less than a year after our ground zero awakening, we renewed our vows in our pastor's office with our two preschoolers as attendants, one holding a bouquet and the other our matching silver bands. The new wedding bands had "He is my beloved and I am his" etched on the outside in Hebrew. On the inside of our rings I chose these words that are meaningful to both of us: "I bought you to set you free."

I had questioned how this good girl would ever see beyond her own pain. But it was in this barren place that I found Jesus.

The most breathtaking moments often come when we discover we have nothing left, but everything we need. This deep brokenness feels like the end, but it's actually a new beginning. Not only did God bring us through our darkest valley, we now share a beautiful testimony of Terrell's freedom and my forgiveness, and the beauty that comes from both.

I like to refer to it now as BC/AC (before confession/after confession) because I believe these devastating moments in our lives can be redeeming. God can use a painful breach of trust in marriage, the heartbreak of an ill child, or a financial blow to bring us back to the basics and remind us how much we need Jesus. The hard seasons make us stronger. Struggling is part of moving forward.

From the depths of brokenness, God had given us something new, something so much better than what we thought we had. It didn't take long for our passion and second honeymoon to lead to another baby on the way. God turned our sorrow into joy.

❊

The day finally came when I had time to reclaim my broken pitcher. With my curious firstborn at my heels, I gathered supplies and took my project to the back porch. "Momma, that's broken," she said, pointing to the colorful pieces of pottery from my beloved pitcher. As I spread mortar on a stone and carefully fit the broken pieces together, I answered, "Yes, it used to be something beautiful, but I broke it."

"Why did it break, Momma?"

"It slipped out of Momma's hand," I said softly.

"Oh," she said.

I looked at the mosaic I was creating on the stone and thought, *It broke because it was too weak to stay together, but now I'm going to make it into something new and beautiful, something stronger.* It was true of both my work of art and our marriage.

After so many years of trying and doing, I ended up with a pile of broken dreams. But that's God's specialty: He loves turning broken things into beauty. When I didn't know what to do or where to go, I learned utter dependence on God. I was broken, then mended together by Him and ready to be used. I was exactly where He wanted me.

❖ ❀ ❋

UNPINNED FAITH

When we break something in our home, our first impulse is to throw it away because it's damaged. In our mind, its value has diminished when it is cracked or in pieces. But it can be transformed into something different, something new. Psalm 147:3 reminds us that God "heals the brokenhearted and binds up their wounds." When we embrace the empty place and cling to God in the valley, we find streams in the desert that lead us to God. It's there that we are able to thank Him for the brokenness and the new opportunities that come with it. Sometimes we heal stronger.

Telling you about this "ground zero moment" in my life wasn't easy.

I couldn't imagine God taking the broken pieces of my life and repurposing them for His glory, putting me in a position of saying yes to whatever He asked. But that's exactly what He was about to do.

Be honest with yourself: What are you struggling with today? How can you turn what you are wrestling with into an opportunity for growth and strength?

Change your perspective: view brokenness as a place to find God. Look for the beauty in barrenness.

———— ❋ ————

CHAPTER 4

THE SWEET SPOT

---- ✳ ----

The greatest moments in life are the miraculous moments when
human impotence and divine omnipotence intersect.

MARK BATTERSON

I APPLIED PRESSURE to my son's mouth, afraid to pull back the bloody towel wrapped in ice. I knew Jon-Avery would survive his latest injury, but sitting in the emergency room, I was still shaken by the sight of his blood on my shirt. Even though he had finally calmed down, I wasn't quite there yet.

I should have known the space between the couch and chair in the living room would be too big a temptation for a five-year-old not to swing between the two. He over-rotated and his baby teeth took the brunt of his fall. I was up to my elbows in raw hamburger meat when I heard his screams. I ran, uncooked meat and all, and grew faint at the sight of his dangling front teeth and bruised gums. And mercy, the blood!

Terrell was still at work. Our son's screams got the attention of his big sister and started his baby sister howling too. I put my head between my knees to stop from passing out. I wish I was joking about that. But I decided an unconscious momma wouldn't be helpful. The wooziness passed, and I ran around frantically trying to figure out what to do. In other words, don't call me if there's blood. My sister, Kara, rushed over to stay with the girls while I headed to the emergency room.

Again. For the fifth time that month.

Prior to this there had been kidney stones, a staph infection, a concussion (running child meets freshly mopped floor), dehydration from a stomach bug, and a remote control car antenna to an eyeball. Let's just make it clear: we met our large annual family deductible in January alone.

I walked in and heard "Hello, Mrs. Welch" from the lady behind the desk. I hadn't even had time to sign my name on the waiting list. I reddened at being recognized and wanted the earth to swallow me up. I found a quiet corner to sit down with my son. Pulling back the towel that I had wrapped around his mouth, I winced at his purple, swollen gums. I shook my head and felt a giggle-slash-sob bubble up within me and escape. I believe some call it hysteria. Still, in that moment, I had a life-changing epiphany.

I have always judged those families whose members are constantly getting injured, experiencing some catastrophe, running out of gas, throwing tantrums in the Walmart canned-food aisle—you know the ones. The basically imperfect people. Today—oh my word—*we* were them. *We were THAT family.*

It was a coming-to-grips-with-reality moment as I sat there waiting for our son's name to be called. Here I had always been quick to criticize people for being human when I had a big plank of human sticking out of my own eye. I wasn't better than anyone else. When I recognized myself as one of the people I had judged, I had compassion (okay, self-pity, maybe) and realized, *This is my life. It's crazy, unpredictable, funny, hard, embarrassing, but like it or not, this is it.* I thought of all the broken places, the disappointments and failed expectations. My life wasn't notable or even beautiful most days, but it was mine.

I get it, God. My family and I are normal. I can accept that. Especially because I know that You're there in the midst of it all.

My son was finally treated, and as we left the hospital that day, I thought about my new revelation and my old desire and struggle to be a writer. Six months earlier, I had started a little blog for moms, thanks to my husband's urging.

✳

It had been more than a year since Terrell's confession and our ground zero experience. In that year, we lived and worked and carried on, but we did so as newly older weds. In other words, we had the hots for each other and were simply consumed with love. I remember overhearing my dad say after watching us at lunch one day, "If those two aren't careful, they're going to have another baby."

Everything in my world was clearer, brighter, and more intimate. Life wasn't perfect. We still struggled, especially when the past reminders resurfaced, but for the first time in our marriage, we had the tools to combat them. We learned the great secret that Ruth Bell Graham shared: "A happy marriage is the union of two great forgivers."[1]

Terrell had never known such freedom, and with his eyes only for me, it wasn't long before I was bulging with our third child. She was conceived in forgiveness and freedom and a lot of grace.

It was a difficult pregnancy (by difficult I mean *horrible*), and after months of problems (namely multiple bladder infections turned kidney issues), our baby girl came seven weeks early. Emerson was tiny and spent three weeks in the neonatal intensive care unit learning how to breathe. When she was released to come home, they packed her up with an apnea monitor that would remind her to breathe when she forgot. Terrell and I learned CPR, along with my mom. We showed our other kids the basics and held our own breath a lot of the time. Emerson slept next to our bed for the first six months of her life, and we slept with one eye open, waiting for the alarm to sound. This raw experience for our family of loving a preemie drew us even closer to God and one another.

Since Emerson was born in the dead of winter, I was paranoid she would get sick, compromise her tiny body, and not have enough strength to fight back. So I fell into a routine of welcoming my "big" kids home from school, sanitizing their hands (okay, bodies) at the door, and keeping their newborn sister confined to our bedroom. Once they were germ-free, I tried to let Madison and Jon-Avery bond with Emerson, helping bring diapers, carefully holding her, patting her back to coax a burp, but I felt like I had two families: the healthy ones who carried germs and the fragile one who was susceptible to every one of them. I was a psychotic new mom—for the third time.

As Emerson grew, she got stronger and her little body didn't cause the alarms to sound as often. But by that point I had isolated myself in an unhealthy way. I didn't leave the house unless I had to, and I was exhausted and desperately lonely. I recognized this and so did my husband. If I ran errands, it was at night, when Terrell could do daddy duty. I didn't go to lunch with friends or attend church for months.

Valentine's Day rolled around eight weeks after Emerson was born, and Terrell gave me pearls. I said thank you and mumbled, "Oh, the perfect gift for a shut-in." Clearly, I needed a mental health holiday, and my husband knew it. He didn't let my attitude ruin the night; instead he talked me into going out to dinner with my family at a nearby Mexican restaurant.

It was a disaster from the minute we sat down. The waiter accidentally knocked a glass of iced tea into Emerson's brand-new pink monogrammed diaper bag—the first time I'd taken it out in public except for doctor visits. We sopped up the mess and ordered fajitas. Our son started looking queasy after a few tortilla chips, and I ran to the bathroom with him just in time for him to cover two stalls with lunch, breakfast, and well, you get the point. He continued to be sick all over the bathroom. I was so stunned by the sudden turn of events that I was crying and laughing at the same time. We ended up wrapping Jon-Avery in Emerson's new blanket, carrying him out to the car, and eating our cold fajitas at home. This little night out took me weeks to get over. But the months of isolation were pushing me toward the place I needed to go and where God wanted me to be.

✻

One day Terrell brought home a laptop and said, "I think you need to write." I had spent the first five years of our marriage before kids attending writing conferences, participating in critique groups, and submitting proposals with very little success. But Terrell knew my dream to be a writer, and he knew that awakening that dormant place in me might be just the thing to get me out of the dumps. And so, in my pajamas, quarantined to my bedroom with a baby who was thriving more each day, I started a mom blog, although at the time I didn't even realize that's what it was called. I didn't know anything about blogging. I kept in touch with my friend Robin by reading her family blog, which was the only one I followed. I had no idea I was about to enter a parallel online world. Terrell had given me a Mac, and when I was getting comfortable with its bells and whistles, I saw that you could publish your own website. And that's exactly what I did.

I had two faithful readers (thank you, Mom and Dad). I mostly wrote funny little stories about my kids. I sent out an e-mail to friends and family and invited them to read along. It didn't take me long to realize I'd stumbled into the giant world of blogging. There was a name for what I was doing, and I was hooked. Terrell could see the excitement growing in me and brought home a copy of *Blogging for Dummies*. I read it cover-to-cover.

Before starting my blog, I hadn't written a word in nearly eight years. That's a long time for a writer to be quiet. It's also hard to call yourself a writer when you don't write. But a dormant dream doesn't mean you're not a dreamer. I didn't write because I was living the story, storing up words like the broken pieces of the pitcher in my life. I didn't know God was about to fit them together to create a new mosaic.

When I wrote those first words on a screen—a riveting story about our first tooth fairy visit—I felt like I'd come home. I was doing something that made me feel alive. I was unleashing a dream that I thought had died.

But six months later, when I sat in that hospital emergency room with my son, I was still portraying us superficially, writing to present a neat picture of our happy little home. I was writing what I thought people wanted to read. And honestly? It wasn't really working. As I drove home from the hospital that day with my toothless son, I knew I was being called to authenticity. It was time to get real. It was time to write for myself to an audience of One. Learning how to blog had become an unpaid part-time job for me in between caring for my kids. Not only was I writing, I was interacting with other moms with comments and through social media. I discovered I wasn't alone: I had found a community.

I revamped my blog and called it *We are THAT family . . . you know the ones.*

I started writing about the mess of my life. I pushed back the curtain and showed the chaos. Instead of trying to change my life or pretend it was better than it was, I decided to accept it. And that actually made the mess beautiful. I found unexpected freedom and love for the life God had given me, bloody and dirty as it might be.

❋

At church one night, I felt a stirring to dedicate my writing to God, praying, "Lord, I ask You to take my words and use them for Your glory. I pray that I would say what You want me to and that it will touch others." I had no idea where my prayer would take me. I made the conscious decision to write for His glory, not my own, because He totally gets motherhood, poop and puke included.

There wasn't a great master plan or goal to start something big. I hit "publish" on my first blog post with the new name, and in that simple yes, I discovered my sweet spot. My first *real* post was called "The Magic Eraser." I shared the story about discovering my kids coloring with permanent markers at our new dining room table. I realized the markers had bled through the paper, staining our wood table. I freaked out, and after yelling at them, sent them to their rooms. Then I remembered the Magic Eraser sponge under the sink and scrubbed the ugly stains away. I felt guilty for overreacting and called the kids downstairs. My blog post on June 29, 2008, told the rest of the story:

> "I was wrong. I made a mistake. I shouldn't have let you use those markers or I should have put a tablecloth down first. I'm sorry for yelling and blaming you. It was not your fault. Can you forgive me?" My daughter shrugged and my son sniffled.
>
> "I sinned," I confessed. They both looked up at me. Surprise registered on their faces.
>
> I took the Magic Eraser and pretended to rub it all over my body.
>
> "What are you doing?" my daughter asked in a horrified voice.
>
> "I'm erasing myself. I don't feel like a very good mom right now," I answered. There was a smile.
>
> "I forgive you," my daughter said.
>
> "Me, too," my son said.
>
> They left me standing in the kitchen. I picked up the eraser to put it away. I still felt bad. Angry for being so human. I looked at the eraser and wished I could swipe it across my heart to remove the awful residue.
>
> And then I remembered I can. We make mistakes. We feel bad, even sorry. We ask forgiveness. The sin is wiped away, just like that. The Magic Eraser. I got to use two of them in one day. And I am thankful for both.

My venture into the world of blogging was accidental in so many ways but it was also providential. It was the divine collision of intimacy with God, timing, hard work, skills, and passion. I was talking to God. I was a lonely mom. I needed an outlet. I loved writing and I had the time to pursue it. In doing so, I discovered a passion to encourage other moms just like me.

So after more than a decade of dreaming of being a writer, I finally decided to become one. Saying yes was more about courage and faith than opportunity and success. I don't think we always recognize our God-sized dream for what it is, especially when it's wrapped up in our normalcy. I could identify with what writer Ann Voskamp said: "You were made for the place where your real passion meets compassion, because there lies your real purpose."[2] I stopped listening to the voice of rejection, threw out the old file folder full of rejection letters I'd been hanging on to from my first writing endeavors, and stepped out into the perfect intersection to meet God and embark on a new chapter of my life.

<hr>

My sweet spot wasn't exactly a success story. I think we often confuse glory with something glorious. Nothing really changed, not for a long time. But *I* had changed. I was pursuing my passion. I was living an authentic life. I was satisfied, and that changed everything.

I discovered that the one thing we are called to do—our mission—is really secondary. It's found only after we pursue the primary, the ultimate goal of our lives, which is to bring glory to God. This is our foundational, primary mission and purpose for living. It is what we were created for. Isaiah 43:6-7 says we were made by God for His glory.

Sean Eppers, one of the pastors at my church, explained it this way: There aren't two paths in the lives we've been given—one for us to pursue our dreams, the other to serve God. When we divide up our lives into those compartments, we work for our glory, not His. But when our lives flow with the central purpose of shining *His* light, it gives us deep satisfaction and contentment, and leads us directly to the secondary. I have found John Piper's statement to be true: "God is most glorified in us when we are most satisfied in him."[3]

Our primary job is to have a relationship with Jesus. It's the only way to discover the contentment in life we all crave. And when we focus on intimacy with God, He provides the right timing, coupling it with our hard work and skills, and passion is born.

I worked hard at becoming a blogger. I found the vulnerability uncomfortable, the growth slow, the learning curve vast. But I also stumbled upon an online parallel world filled with lonely moms just like me. Most blogs don't gain readers simply because they are on the Internet. It requires a lot of hard work—consistently good writing; finding your unique voice (there are actually thousands of blogs to choose from, and it's easy to be just another one); and faithfulness. It also requires interaction with other bloggers. I attended my first blogging conference in February 2009. I was scared to fly and actually meet women I'd only known through comments and blogging.

Terrell bought me a cute outfit for the trip and I kissed my kids good-bye, and when I got to the conference I made deep friendships that I still hold dear today. Then I came home and I wrote and wrote and wrote some more, publishing more than a thousand blog posts and growing a committed readership.

This space stretched me and provided a community of many other families who spent just as much time as we did in the emergency room.

Our sweet spots may look different from those of others. But whatever you find yourself doing—mothering, being a wife, or chasing a career—do it unto God.

Because where you're living today is the place where God has put you. He orders our steps, even when we misstep. Sometimes this place isn't where we want to be. It's uncomfortable and challenging, and it doesn't feel like our dream. There are valleys on the journey to the mountaintop.

I look at my husband, who left full-time ministry nearly a decade ago. Terrell gets up at 4:30 a.m. most days, dresses in the dark so he won't disturb me, goes to the fitness club, and pushes his body to its limits with a grueling hour-long CrossFit workout before returning home to get ready for work. He endures this regimen as part of his fight against diabetes. He lets me sleep in as long as possible. I often awake to the sound of bathwater that he runs for me or hearing him rummaging through the pantry making school lunches and encouraging the kids to get ready for the day.

I am married to a good man, a pastor who had to reinvent himself as a sales representative when we left full-time ministry. He is smart and hardworking. And his daily faithfulness to the mundane takes my breath away.

In my eyes, Terrell is still a pastor. He shepherds our family. He prays with coworkers and shines for Jesus in his work. He is a light in a dark world, and more and more he is finding his sweet spot.

Is it his dream to be a sales rep? No. But Terrell is faithful to the primary—glorifying God with his life. I believe with all my heart that when the time is right, God will merge this with Terrell's secondary, the big dream we are still too afraid to say out loud. My husband is being faithful to the now. And his obedience isn't small in God's eyes. I like how author and blogger Holley Gerth puts it: "What you're doing isn't small if it's what God has for you. It's big. And it just may lead to something bigger."[4]

It has been a challenging road for Terrell and our family. One with turns and obstacles we didn't expect, something John Piper has described well:

> Life is not a straight line leading from one blessing to the next and then finally to heaven. Life is a winding and troubled road. Switchback after switchback. And the point of biblical stories like Joseph and Job and Esther and Ruth is to help us feel in our bones (not just know in our heads) that God is for us in all these strange turns. God is not just showing up after the trouble and cleaning it up. He is plotting the course and managing the troubles with far-reaching purposes for our good and for the glory of Jesus Christ.[5]

Jesus has been with us down every path, and as we dream of the future and ask God for direction, His invisible hand guides us. We continue on for His glory.

I am not a patient person. I hate waiting—in line, at the mailbox, on God. But often God puts us in this uncomfortable spot because it's where the hard work is done. When God says wait, it's because He's getting ready to show up. The road to my sweet spot was marked with many not-so-sweet experiences, but because of them I understood more of the journey.

Hindsight is enlightening. God rewards faithfulness. Here's what I'm learning about finding my sweet spot as I watch my husband discover his:

God uses our brokenness for His purpose.
What He puts back together heals stronger.
Loving people is a full-time ministry.
(Title, position, and pay are not necessary.)
There are setbacks and tragedies in our journey.
God plots our course for His glory.

❋

A few months after the blogging conference, Terrell and I were on a coffee date at Starbucks. We knew it was going to be a good night when we scored the big comfy chairs tucked away in the corner. My husband and I curled up with our lattes and did something we've never done before: we dreamstormed.

"It's sort of like brainstorming," my husband said excitedly. "Except instead of writing down ideas, we're writing down our dreams. The wilder, bigger, and crazier, the better."

We didn't hold back. Some of the things on our list included working together again someday, starting a business so we could focus more on ministry, and traveling internationally as a family.

Dreamstorming is a great exercise for your brain. Normally, our brains automatically zero in on all of the impossibilities we might face if we step out in faith and obedience. With dreamstorming, the impossible is replaced with the possible. It's amazing for us to look back at that list from years ago and see a few of the things coming to pass now. Let's face it: God likes to show off.

Your sweet spot isn't some elusive mystery that God dangles

over your head just beyond your grasp. It's the collision of believing in who you are and acting on it because of whom you belong to.

Little did I know that my sweet spot, a place that had become familiar, comfortable, and safe, was about to lead me to a yes I could have never imagined. But that's how God works: when we live for Him one yes at a time, He rewrites our story.

UNPINNED FAITH

God has a unique purpose for you. Your yes won't look like anyone else's yes; it will be completely one-of-a-kind, just like you. Beth Moore explains it perfectly: "Who are you supposed to look like in your calling here on earth and in the way you follow Christ? You're supposed to look like the version of you that loves Jesus with everything in you."[6]

That's the real you.

And that's the road on which you will find what He put you on the planet to do. You don't have to figure out what to surrender to. Just surrender your heart to Jesus. Every single ounce of it. Ask Him to give you a love for Him that surpasses anything in your human experience, a supernatural capacity. Ask Him for it every day until He does it, and then ask Him to do it some more.

If you're a writer, your exploding love for Him will bring it out. If you're a liberator, you will not be able to keep yourself from fighting to free the oppressed. If you're a teacher, you won't be able to quit studying except to share what you learned with somebody. If you love Him with your whole heart and that whole heart says sell everything and move to a third-world country, girl, get your passport!

Live Matthew 22:37: "Love the Lord your God with all your heart and with all your soul and with all your mind."

I encourage you to set aside some quality time to get to know yourself and what your sweet spot may be. Here are a few questions to ask yourself to begin the process:

- What is the world's greatest need?
- How would I solve it?
- What is the one thing I need to do?
- What subjects do I love reading about?
- What would I do for free? (List everything that you can think of.)
- What comes easily and naturally to me?
- At the end of a long day, what's the thing that I've done that brings me satisfaction?
- What would I regret never doing?
- When close friends or family think of me, what would they say my passion is? (If you don't know the answer, ask them.)
- What do I love about myself?
- What is stopping me from doing the thing I love?
- Am I afraid to take a risk? If so, what is holding me back? (Be honest with yourself.)

CHAPTER 5

THE DAY I WOKE UP

※

I avoided coming to visit the poor . . . for a long time.
I was afraid my heart would be broken by their condition.
Instead, today, I found my heart broken by my condition.

KEN DAVIS

I'LL NEVER FORGET the day I went to hell.

I was nervous as armed guards walked me, a group of other bloggers, and our guides down a muddy trail that descended into a quarry walling in the dangerous area known as Mathare Valley. We had been invited by Compassion International to blog about one of Kenya's largest slums, where 700,000 people live in a three-square-mile area. That's comparable to squeezing more than sixteen thousand people onto a football field.

The night before, we had been briefed by Shaun Groves, our trip leader, on what to expect on our first visit to Mathare. We would be on foot, protected by guards as we headed into the heart of the slum. We were instructed to leave our cameras and computers at the hotel because it was too great a risk to take them in. I couldn't eat anything after our briefing and had a restless night. It was hard not to be afraid.

The slum has no police or fire stations within its perimeters and no paved roads. The police in Nairobi, about three miles away, are not allowed to enter the area, which makes it one of the most dangerous places in the country.

The slum is known for extreme poverty and orphan-led homes. The typical house is a six-by-eight-foot tin shanty (the size of the rug under my dining room table) that is held together by mud; some houses just have cardboard roofs and walls. We were told by our guides that homes didn't have electricity or running water or, in some cases, even beds to sleep on. The green stream that snaked its way through the slum was more sewage than water; it was regularly used as a public toilet.

It was raining the day we visited. The wet "ground" wasn't dirt at all; it was made of trampled garbage, several feet deep. I smelled the stench coming from plastic bags filled with human waste long before I saw them floating in the green river. (The bags are nicknamed "flying toilets," tossed into the Nairobi River under the cover of darkness, even though the river is the main water supply for the people who live there.) In my wildest imagination, I could never have conjured up the images I now can't forget.

I couldn't stop shaking as I kept up with the group of bloggers. I was trembling from more than fear; it was the palpable darkness, hopelessness, and oppression everywhere I looked. I covered my mouth and nose with the scarf I was wearing to stop gagging.

Besides the toxic stench of the river, there was a sickeningly sweet scent in the air. "What do I smell?" I asked one of our guides.

He pointed to a staggering drunk and said, "Some 'industrious' men brew their own alcohol called *chang'aa*, which means 'kill me quick' in Swahili. It's a popular, often lethal cocktail of distilled grains. Some distillers add a kick of jet fuel or battery acid to the drink." I shook my head, trying to comprehend.

We passed a couple of teenage boys holding white bottles between their teeth. "Glue boys," one of our leaders said quietly. "They squelch their hunger pains by getting high on the fumes from factory glue." He grabbed my hand and pulled me along. "Let's keep going," he said, adding what encouraging words he could.

But the farther I walked, the more I saw. Children along the path called out to us—the white visitors. I had been keeping my eyes on the path, watching where I was stepping in hopes of dodging the raw sewage squishing under my shoes, but now I looked up at the small, half-dressed children. They were unsmiling, filthy, and looked sickly. Flies hovered around their noses and eyes, and they had swollen bellies and listless faces. "How-ah-you? How-ah-you?" I listened to their high-pitched, innocent voices, repeating the same words over and over with palms upturned, begging for money. One child's cough was as deep as a death rattle. I had to look away.

These living conditions were not for the *living*.

The streets were crowded not only with countless children but also young prostitutes. I saw a scantily dressed young girl, trying to look appealing, on the corner. But she was really just a child who looked hungry and desperate. One of our guides had mentioned how rampant AIDS is here—one out of three people was HIV positive. *I wonder if she is one of them?* Drug use and alcohol abuse were common among young and old alike. People were sitting everywhere, most of them with a vacant stare. *What are they waiting for?* Extension cords lay in muddy water, snaking their way from generators into small pornography shacks to power televisions showing salacious videos.

I didn't want to look at another desperate face. Once again, I concentrated on my feet. I began to cry and couldn't stop. My tears splashed my shoes and mixed with the sorrow of this hellhole.

At every turn, I only saw hopelessness. I wanted to shut it all out. I was so angry and silently accused God. *Where are You? These are Your people; You created them. How can You allow so much suffering?*

For a moment, time stood still. I stopped and closed my eyes. I saw God's finger pointed at my chest as He asked my spirit the same question: *"Kristen, how can* you *allow this?"*

In that exact moment, I knew my life would never be the same.

Some small decisions are big right from the word yes. In 2010, when Compassion International invited me to be one of several guest bloggers to write about poverty in Kenya, it definitely got my attention. Over the years, the relief organization has found that these firsthand experiences in third-world and developing countries described in blogs help readers start thinking about sponsoring children living in extreme conditions. When I received the invitation, I told Terrell, "There is no way I can do this." I knew I would be traveling way out of my comfort zone, and my comfort zone was, well, comfy. Terrell just smiled and encouraged me to at least consider it.

Now that I was in the midst of it, I couldn't help but think, *How exactly did I get here?*

Oh. Yes. I had said yes.

And Terrell was partly to blame.

For the previous nine months, my husband had been on his own journey of abandoning the status quo. He had been listening to podcasts by pastor David Platt, who challenges American Christians to examine what they have in comparison to the majority of the world and embrace what really counts the most and grows the Kingdom of God. It isn't money or possessions or status. It's being obedient and willing to say to God, "I will do anything and sacrifice everything to spread your Good News to the ends of the earth." What David Platt was saying shook up Terrell's own dream of bigger and better and more for our family. He was beginning to ask hard questions and dream crazy dreams.

One day he said, "I've been thinking. Do we really need to stockpile money in our savings account, 401(k), and college fund? What if God wants us to give that money to people in need? Or at least be willing to do so."

This kind of talk made me uncomfortable. Terrell's new mind-set terrified me. "I like having a savings account. It makes me feel secure."

When I finally told Compassion I would go, only half the battle was over. As I filled out papers and applied for my passport, I worried and fretted and came up with a lot of excuses. "God, I have small children to take care of and Africa is, well, *Africa*. What if I can't handle it? What if something happens to me or to my family while I'm away?" (I forgot that He already knew these things.) I was also starting to think more seriously about what Terrell had been thinking about. I was fulfilled as a wife, mother, and writer, but deep down, I was dissatisfied with my excess.

Somewhere along the way I had gotten off track, and I spent

a lot of time and money pursuing trivial things. And the more I acquired, the emptier I felt. I knew God hadn't healed the broken places in my life for shallow, unfulfilled living. And while I was doing small things here and there for Him and trying to be an encouragement to young moms through my writing, I wanted more. I wanted to make a difference in the world. I wanted my life to matter, to be part of something bigger than me. I wanted my life to be about Jesus.

A few weeks after I said yes to going to Africa, my family gathered around me after dinner one night. They had a gift for me. I wrote about it on my blog:

FEBRUARY 8, 2010

I once had a dream of making a Christian T-shirt to wear to school. I came up with a design after school hours on the computer. My idea: an upside-down world that said, "I want to turn the world upside down for Jesus."

I wanted to do something hard.

When I told my daughter about it, she couldn't believe I'd never had that shirt made. It just wasn't an easy thing back then. I wasn't sure she'd gotten the point of my story.

I hadn't thought about that young girl I used to be in a long time. I went to bed feeling discouraged that I couldn't even get caught up on laundry or get my toddler to eat her dinner, much less change the world.

Well, something amazing happened this past week:

I got my shirt!!

My unbelievable hubby created it online and surprised me with it.

Y'all, I cried when I read the front:

"I want to turn the world upside down for Jesus."
—Kristen, age 14

I haven't even gone to Africa yet and my life is being turned upside down.

It's a new, uncomfortable place—that feels right.

As I packed and prepared to leave, I was so emotional. I had never been away from my family that long. But my husband and children offered their support in so many ways and encouraged me when I was full of doubt.

FEBRUARY 16, 2010

I think I've made it clear that I'm married to an amazing guy. Not only is he the bravest man I know, he's a quiet artist. He delights our kids with his unbelievable Play-Doh sculptures and pencil portraits and occasionally keeps himself awake in church sketching our pastor. (I never said he was perfect.)

He has an eye for color and loves making things with his hands.

With a bit of copper, a dab of silver, and more love than I deserve, he made a necklace for me for Valentine's Day.

He sculpted the copper into the shape of Africa and stamped the word *upendo* across the center, which means "love" in Swahili.

Saying good-bye to my family, getting on the plane, and flying halfway around the world with people I didn't know stretched me beyond myself, and I hadn't even stepped onto foreign soil yet. My kids wrote me notes for each day of my trip. I read them all in the airport and cried a river before the plane ever took off. I carried their words with me: "Dear Mommy, I am so proud of you. I will miss you so much." I'm an introvert and a scaredy-cat, and this yes was the hardest of my life (so far).

But I decided to undertake what would turn out to be a gut-wrenching, painful journey because I wanted to tell the story of the people who were living it every day. What I didn't know was that I was going to be rescued and rewritten in the process.

❋

I immediately got in the shower when I returned to my tiny hotel room after that first day in the slum. The scalding water ran down my shoulders, and I braced myself against the wall as sobs racked my body. I had seen so much in a short time, and I didn't know what to do with it. I poured out my heart to God, something that would become a daily process. I was alone in Africa but not lonely. I asked Him hard questions, and He asked them back. He reminded me that He was there in the heart of Mathare Valley.

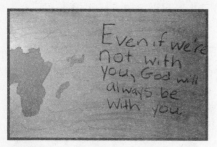

One of the notes from my kids that made me cry

He was right. I had seen it with my own eyes—an oasis in the middle of the slum. It was a compound that housed the Compassion International project. Inside, we met the most beautiful children in the world. They wore neat uniforms and had smudge-free faces. *Do they really live in the slum?* They seemed so out of place. Their smiles lit up the room as they sang and danced. I wanted to take off my shoes because it was holy ground.

One of our tour guides, Maureen Owino, was a recent graduate of Compassion's sponsorship program. She had grown up in unimaginable poverty just like we were seeing. I pulled her aside, desperate to understand how she and these children could smile and laugh and possess an inner joy I couldn't fathom.

"Tell me your story," I urged her.

Maureen had grown up in a one-room shack with dirt floors and one bed for six people. "We were the poorest of the poor," she said. "Breakfast and lunch were a luxury, and dinner usually consisted of porridge without sugar." She didn't know what it felt like to have a stomach that wasn't rumbling from hunger. Once after going several days without food, she and her sister decided to go look for some in their Nairobi slum. They found rotten vegetables and rotten fruit and thanked God for them. "I was around six years old. It was a breakthrough from starvation," she said. Eventually Maureen was sponsored and grew up in a Compassion program.

It was hard to imagine this confident, beautiful young woman living, let alone starving, in a slum.

"You are from America. Do you know my sponsors?" she asked.

I smiled and told her my country was quite large. "What would you tell your sponsors if you could meet them today?"

"I would tell them I am a hero in my country because of them."

Maureen wore a clean white satin shirt—her best, I later learned. She was the size of my daughter, who was ten at the time, and had walked miles to the project earlier that morning. She was dynamic and strong, a leader whom people followed. *Hero* was the perfect word to describe her. As she finished her remarkable story, I wiped tears from my eyes. Her face exuded joy and peace. And I wanted what she had.

Her next question caught me off guard. "Are you on Face-book?"

I laughed, looking around at our surroundings, and said, "Are you?"

She had Internet access through her university. "In three months I'm coming to America for the first time to travel to camps with a ministry called Student Life and share my story on behalf of Compassion International. Maybe we could meet?"

I jotted down my name on a slip of paper and handed it to her. "I would love that. If you come to my state, maybe I can bring my family to meet you." I knew it was unlikely even as I said it.

Meeting Maureen for the first time

We left the safety of the project and visited the homes of some of the sponsored children, with Maureen leading us as part of her role as a Leadership Development student.

※

Our group stopped at a tiny shanty. I ducked inside a space about the size of a closet. There stood a young boy named Vincent, a sponsored child who was also an orphan and parent to his little brother. While we were standing there, I was startled when water began dripping through the cracks in the tin roof and hitting me in the head. I tried to move out of the way. I blocked out the sounds coming through the walls of the community toilet nearby, one that Vincent and his brother shared with their neighbors. I listened to Vincent tell us how he walked miles to school every day, coming and going in the dark.

Vincent looked so peaceful. The light that radiated from his eyes filled the dark room of his hovel. *How can he be so content with so little?*

I couldn't stop the questions from coming out of my mouth. "Why are you so happy? Why aren't you afraid?"

He looked at me as if I'd missed the point entirely. "Because I have Jesus."

He didn't say anything else. He didn't have to. It was enough.

He was right; I had missed it. Entirely.

I said I lived for Jesus, but the truth was that Jesus really wasn't enough for me. Not like He was for Vincent, Maureen, and the children from the garbage dump who sang about Him and dreamed dreams for the future.

The very thought took my breath away.

It was like an invisible veil had been lifted from my eyes. I saw my life, my home, all the things that screamed success, and they were like dung. This was a painful revelation to me, a Christ-follower for most of my life. But even in that hard moment, I was convinced that all the choices in my life, the road I had journeyed, the broken dreams and broken places, the healing, had led me to this place across the globe for a specific purpose. I missed my family and the comforts of home, but I was on a God-appointed mission, and I knew I was exactly where I needed to be.

When I honestly looked into my heart, I knew I equated Jesus with comfort and blessings. Vincent had nothing except a leaky roof over his head, and yet he was content. I envied him. In a few days I would return to a lifestyle with every convenience and only want more. I added Jesus like salt and pepper to a tasteless dish. He wasn't the main course for me, just an extra on the side.

My happiness in life was always conditional, ready to disappear with every storm that blew into my life. It was contingent upon what I had versus what I wanted. There were always

strings attached.

Vincent's profound statement woke me up from my American Dream.

In that faraway, uncomfortable place, I discovered just how much I needed Jesus

Inside Vincent's home

to be Lord of my life. I had erected so many barriers between us and was so busy pursuing trivial, temporary things that I didn't even recognize the obstacles separating us. I didn't even know I needed to be rescued. I thought I was going to Kenya to help, to give a voice to the voiceless. But I was the one drowning in all that I had. I was the one who needed help. I was the one who was spiritually poor.

I watched Vincent light a small candle stub stuck on a makeshift metal holder, the "lamp" by which he studied and did his homework. I saw the light of Jesus in that dim room. I found redemption.

✳

I have always thought of myself as a compassionate person. Since I was a young girl, I have loved people and wanted to do good. But somewhere along the way in my Christian walk, I'd forgotten the most important thing: *Christ.* I wanted clean compassion, the kind that is more about me feeling good about what I've done, the kind that could be covered by writing a check and not investing anything else. In Africa, the emptiness of my life coincided with the hope that I saw and demanded something I didn't possess. Most of the bloggers on my trip had brought along their spouses. I felt very alone as I tried to process much of this on my own. It forced me to turn to God.

Instead of being filled with anxiety and fear, trembling about the unknown, I was processing all I had seen and experienced. I knew it was going to be a challenge fitting the new me back into my old life.

Redemption comes when we least expect it but exactly when we need it the most: next to a hospital bed, at a birth or death, alone with God or surrounded by friends, or when we say a reluctant yes on foreign soil. God knows exactly how to grab our attention and refocus it on Himself, using ordinary and extraordinary means.

God used a day in hell to rescue me.

⁂

I stuffed two weeks' worth of dirty, dusty laundry into my bag, patted my back pocket for my passport, and got ready to say good-bye to the country that had broken my heart. I was going home a different person. While I didn't really know what that meant for the future, I knew my new perspective of the world, wealth, and poverty had shattered my old views into a thousand pieces. I didn't realize God was breaking me again so I would heal *stronger*, but I did know that my first trip overseas had wrecked me. I was a complete mess—mentally, physically, emotionally, spiritually—and I needed time to sort it all out. In a sense, it would take twice as long to get home from Kenya as it took to get there.

Our group of eleven arrived at the crowded Nairobi airport late at night to catch our long flight back to the stopover in Amsterdam. We had been blogging about our experiences each day on the trip, and the Compassion staff member traveling with us had offered to share with us the number of kids sponsored through each of our blogs. I had avoided asking about my tally all week, relieved that the pressure of "live blogging" was finally over. Day after day, I had been completely focused; I knew I was on a mission from God. I didn't need a number to prove a job well done. Still, as I stood in line to check my bag, curiosity got the best of me. I longed to know if my hard work and words had been effective. I knew more than a thousand kids had been sponsored during our trip.

So I asked.

"Forty-six."

I tried not to show my disappointment.

"That's forty-six lives rescued from poverty, Kristen," Chris Giovagnoni, the social media director of Compassion, said encouragingly. "And many more will probably still be sponsored even after you get home."

I wish I had never asked because there isn't a number that would have been enough. While there was absolutely no pressure from Compassion to get a certain number of kids sponsored, I knew it was costly to take a trip like this, and I wanted the team to feel that they'd made a good decision in inviting me to come. I had written my heart out, but I was still disappointed at the initial results.

At the airline ticket counter, our trip leader learned that I had been bumped to a different airline, along with another couple from our group. Instead of Amsterdam, we were heading to

London, courtesy of Kenyan Airlines. I'm not a world traveler. I am not brave. And I'd never felt more alone in my life.

I sat down in a cramped hallway of the dimly lit terminal on the other side of the world and called home on my cell phone, at three dollars a minute. I updated Terrell on my new travel itinerary, doing my best not to sob into the phone. I wanted to have a pity party right there, next to the burka-clad woman sitting beside me. I was in a foreign place, trying hard to keep it together. I missed my family so much that I couldn't get to them fast enough. For the first time since I'd left home, I wondered if it had all been worth it.

Forty-six. The number kept pounding in my head. It definitely didn't meet the expectations I'd placed on myself. That mind-set wasn't healthy for the long, lonely flight home.

I boarded the cramped plane and found myself wedged in the middle of a long row of people who didn't speak my language or wear deodorant. It was after midnight, and I slept fitfully. I woke up halfway through the eight-hour flight, drenched in sweat and in a full-blown panic attack. As I panted and prayed, I talked myself off the ledge of hysteria by promising myself I would never do this again. I had said my yes to God, had taken care of the assignment, and now I just wanted to return to the safety of my home and family.

From London to Houston, Texas, I relived every single moment of the trip. By the time I arrived in customs twenty-four hours later, I wasn't the strong, semi-brave girl who had left American soil to go change the world. I returned broken, disappointed, and ashamed—I had already forgotten it wasn't all about me.

I made my way to the baggage area, holding my breath the

entire time because I was on the verge of crumbling. When I walked through the sliding glass doors to my waiting family, my just-turned-three-year-old spotted me and ran into my arms. I scooped her up and held her close, finally exhaling. I looked at the others standing there. My older daughter had a homemade card, my son held a bouquet of flowers, and Terrell clutched a gift bag. My parents were there too, smiling and telling me how proud they were. I hugged each of them. When my husband pushed the bag under my nose, I shook my head no.

"It's just a candle and some lotion," Terrell said, confused at my reaction. "We are so proud of you and wanted to get you something."

"Honey, could you please return them? I'm not a hero, and I can't be rewarded for what I've seen and experienced."

He couldn't mask his disappointment, and I felt bad that I had hurt his feelings. It would be the first of many clashes between the new me and the old.

For the first time since I was a teenager with a world-changing agenda, I was dreaming again. I could clearly see that God was going to use all the broken pieces of my life—from high school, marriage, parenting, and beyond—to create something new. He was calling me to make my life about Him, and I knew beyond a shadow of doubt that my biggest yes was yet to come.

❋ ❋ ❋

UNPINNED FAITH

When I think about the beauty and brokenness that make up my life, it's that moment in the slum—standing in Vincent's home, where I realized Jesus wasn't enough for me—that is my defining moment. It's the moment of redemption for me. It wasn't my day of salvation, but it was the day I became third. I decided I wanted to love God first and others second and make myself third.

Have you had any moments like this? My favorite verse since I was a young child has been Romans 12:1-2, and standing in the slum that day, I decided to live it.

So here's what I want you to do, God helping you: Take your everyday, ordinary life—your sleeping, eating, going-to-work, and walking-around life—and place it before God as an offering. Embracing what God does for you is the best thing you can do for him. Don't become so well-adjusted to your culture that you fit into it without even thinking. Instead, fix your attention on God. You'll be changed from the inside out. Readily recognize what he wants from you, and quickly respond to it. Unlike the culture around you, always dragging you down to its level of immaturity, God brings the best out of you, develops well-formed maturity in you. (*The Message*)

I urge you to offer your life, your body, your dreams, your brokenness to Jesus today. It's the highest act of worship.

CHAPTER 6

GIVING BIRTH
TO A DREAM

<hr>

If you've never had a God-sized dream that scared you half to death,
then you haven't really come to life. If you've never been overwhelmed
by the impossibility of your plans, then your God is too small.

MARK BATTERSON

I RETURNED HOME a different person. I knew what I had experienced demanded a response. And a new normal. The next few weeks I felt disoriented, trying to navigate my way back into my family after experiencing such a radical change. What would normal look like for our family now? I didn't know what God wanted from me, but I knew He had set me on a new path.

That first week home I was so emotional. Tears would come while I was cooking dinner because I would remember the children who had no food. I would weep while I ran my kids' bathwater because I had seen how a widow in a remote village had carried water for miles. I would disappear into my room and kneel down next to my bed and sob. I cried for the people I had met, and I cried for me.

I was so relieved to be home again with my family, but home felt different. Long into those first new nights home, Terrell would hold and comfort me. He reminded me of what I knew to be true: if my traipsing across the globe had changed one life, it was enough. He was patient and loving, trying to understand the new woman he was holding.

"Nothing makes sense," I would say. It was so hard not to compare how others lived with how I lived. I was trying to make the two fit together. I had taken so much for granted, and I had so much. I knew God loved me, but I also knew He loved the people I'd met who had nothing.

"Let's start with what does make sense, okay? Let's just take a small step. What feels right today?" he gently asked.

I had just seen the behind-the-scenes operation of Compassion International, and I told him how proud I was to work with them. "I believe in what Compassion is doing. When I met Ephantus and Makena, two of our sponsored kids, and saw the letters we'd written them, some of their most-prized possessions, I knew this organization was the real deal. Honey, sponsoring kids makes sense to me," I said. And for the first time since I'd returned, I felt excited.

❀

In the weeks after I returned from Kenya, I started to sort out my thoughts in my blog posts.

MARCH 14, 2010

I keep thinking about Vincent. I cannot reconcile his lack of every basic need and such fullness in his heart and life. The two don't mix. In America, in my town, in my home and heart,

I complain about a dirty house, yard work, needing a "break" from cooking, or my children. Every basic need is met, PLUS more luxuries than I can count. With so much, how can my joy be incomplete?

How is it that I can see true peace in one of the largest slums in the world, where the smell of death is prominent, and it's rare in the most blessed nation? I'm not sure how to mix these worlds together; how to show my spouse all that I've seen and all that my heart holds, or parent my kids without guilt.

I don't know how to find myself again. I don't know how to return to my everyday life while children still need to be sponsored. But I'm trying. I am so thankful for this place. Although foreign and uncomfortable, I'm not alone. God is right here with me, leading me into new places.

I may be out of Africa, but it will never be out of me.

MARCH 20, 2010

I can see clearly that I've become like my culture, living for myself, my family. Wasting a lot of time and money on things that simply don't matter to me anymore. Choosing ignorance over truth. Pretending poverty isn't my problem or my responsibility.

I've asked God to reveal a new normal, to take this personal revelation and my everyday life and mix them together, creating something entirely different. And I've given Him the heavy burden that comes with such a revelation. His burden is easy and His yoke is light, so it's a pretty good exchange for me.

Terrell was a mess while I was in Kenya, letting God do a good work in him. Turns out we just make a giant mess together!

What does all this look like practically? Well. Less for us, more for others. We had a family meeting and talked openly with our kids. We asked their opinions and talked about Matthew 25:31-46 and what that might mean for our family. (It's also probably not a coincidence that after working diligently to be debt free, as of this week, we don't have a car payment anymore. We just didn't know God already had plans for that money.)

Children are amazing. They voiced their own ideas and concerns and thoughts. I think they naturally want to give; they just usually follow the lead of their parents. Ouch.

APRIL 30, 2010

I've been home from Africa for nearly two months. I probably should be "over" my trip now, back to my old self. Living the life I left.

But I'm not the same. I don't ever want to be the same again. I don't really know where God is leading me (and my family), but it's far away from the person I was two months ago.

I'm discovering that my materialism is layered like an onion . . . layer one has been removed, but I think I'm just getting started on clearing out the stuff (in my home and heart).

I thought I had stuff; turns out, it had me.

I want Christ. He is much greater than all the riches of the world. He fills empty places. And cleans up cluttered hearts.

✳

Just weeks before my trip, we had requested an international adoption packet from America World Adoption Association. My twin sister, Kara, and her family had adopted a precious little girl from Ethiopia the year before. We had fallen in love with her and seen the beauty of adoption firsthand. It had my children urging us to do the same, and many of our friends had grown their families in the same way. We knew we wanted to help orphans in extreme poverty, and honestly, this seemed like the only real option to do so.

But then I went to Africa and met Susan outside of Nairobi. She was an orphan who lived with her grandmother and four other orphaned cousins; she was fortunate to be part of one of the Compassion projects. Compassion, with the help of the child's sponsor, had helped Susan's grandmother start a business that not only provided for this unconventional family, it kept them together. Even in the midst of extreme deprivation according to most people's standards, Susan seemed happy and whole. I couldn't get her smiling face out of my mind. Deep

Susan and me

down, I wanted to see this kind of orphan care flourish, and I longed to be a part of it, even though I had no idea what that meant. It was a scary and exciting idea at the same time.

Don't get me wrong. I admire people who adopt children from other countries. It is the right choice for many people (my dear sister included), but it is expensive. *Is this what you want our family to do, God?* As we prayed and asked hard questions, I knew one thing for sure—for the same $45,000 we were willing to spend to bring one child into our family, we could sponsor ten children through Compassion International for the next twelve years. At a time when nothing in the world made sense to me, that did. And so less than a week after my trip, we sold our little pop-up camper, withdrew money from our savings account, and paid off our minivan so we could free up monthly money. The five of us gathered around my laptop and chose seven more precious children to sponsor, adding to the three we were already sponsoring, many of them orphaned or in HIV-affected areas of the world.

When we began the application process for an international adoption, we had shared the news with some family and friends. It was a huge decision, and we wanted the support of our community. But after we had decided as a family to use the money for sponsoring multiple children instead, we knew we would have to announce we might not adopt after all. Awkward. Because who does that? When we closed the international adoption folder on our desk the night we sponsored seven more kids, we grieved (saying it out loud was extremely difficult to do). It felt like we had lost a child, but we knew we were following our hearts.

"I feel like this is just the beginning," I said.

"Me too," Terrell agreed.

He stood up and started to walk away, but he turned and said, "What else feels right?"

I'll never forget my answer: "Africa feels right. It feels like we are supposed to do something there to help a lot of people."

And as vague and crazy as it sounds, *that was all we had*. But it was enough. My loving husband smiled and peace filled my heart. "Okay. Let's pray and ask God for the next step."

We didn't have any other clues or leads, but there was one saving grace: Terrell and I were in the same place. He was excited about the unknown and believed God had sent me to Africa so that when I returned we'd be on the same radical page—ready to wake up from the American Dream.

I continued to write and process on my blog.

JUNE 9, 2010

I like plans. Carefully laid plans that go perfectly, um, *planned*.

I work hard at organizing my home, the budget, my blog, my life. When I'm at Point A, I define Point B and take the best route there. Lately, nothing has gone as planned. And I know that's how life is at times.

But this time it's different.

Africa happened and I changed, my life and plans right along with it. I don't even know what Point B is anymore. Our family is on an uncertain journey and I don't know where it will lead.

This week, we've pushed aside our organized life, and we've opened our hearts and future to the possibility of something we would have thought insane six months ago.

Getting to this point hasn't been easy. I've fretted and worried money into reserve, and now I just give it away. I've hoarded and decorated, and now I don't care. I've tried to make sense of this new, unexpected journey.

The other night as I soaked in the tub and tried to clear my mind, crowded with thoughts of an uncertain future, I heard these words:

enjoy the journey

Enjoy The Journey

ENJOY THE JOURNEY

Point A and B are destinations; it's the getting there, the place in-between, where we grow and *live*. It was exactly what I needed to hear: *enjoy the journey*. . . . I am.

Deep down I knew God was calling us to something radical. And even though *radical* terrified me, I was more afraid of not following God. When I had followed Him into Kenya, I'd never

felt more alive or closer to Him. Radical was an unknown, and
we had no idea what it might look like.

❋

Over the next few days, an e-mail I'd received from a fellow
blogger two weeks after I'd returned from my trip kept running
through my mind. It contained a link to a CNN article about
one of the slums we had visited in Kenya, the one where God
had spoken to me. The reporter had interviewed the mother
of a young teenage daughter named Beatrice, who had tragically died from a botched abortion. When her father died from
AIDS, Beatrice became a prostitute to provide money for her
family. Her mother was unaware of what her daughter was
doing. And then the teenager got pregnant. She was afraid to
tell her mother and decided to take matters into her own hands.
Abortions are illegal in Kenya, but backstreet solutions are easy
to find in the slum. Beatrice found someone to take care of the
problem with a knitting needle. Not long after, the young girl,
whose mother described her as such a happy child, died of an
infection, one of many girls just like her who prostituted themselves for food and died from abortions gone wrong.[1]

This was the first time I'd read the article, and I cried as I
read the words. I traced the picture of the alley with my finger
and wondered if I had walked that same dirty path. I couldn't
sleep. I had to know if this is how some girls really live in the
country I had fallen in love with.

After a sleepless night, I thought of Maureen, the only person I knew in Kenya. I sent her a message on Facebook with a
link to the CNN article, and I asked her if it was true. "Is this
really what happens in the slum?"

She responded the next day, "Oh my, yes, this article is very true. It's a terrible problem. I even know some former classmates who are living this way."

Without thinking twice, I said, "Can you find someone—a church or group—who helps girls in this situation? I'd like to send them some money." Maureen told me she would.

I'd like to say the next step for our family was clear and direct and easy. But we were about to enter four of the hardest months of our lives. We were in that in-between place, desperate to say yes to God but not knowing the exact question. With the help of Google, we researched organizations and pursued every open door we could find that pointed us toward helping people in Africa. None of them seemed to be what we felt God was calling us to do. We read *When Helping Hurts* by Steve Corbett and Brian Fikkert and began to educate ourselves on the culture we felt called to. We wanted to help, but we were so fearful of making mistakes in our ignorance. Corbett and Fikkert address not only physical poverty but being poor in spirit—that's why it takes much more than handouts and donations to alleviate it. Terrell applied for jobs with nonprofits while I searched mission-based organizations, which is all just a fancy way to say we had no idea what to do.

After a couple of months, we had narrowed down our options to Mercy Ships, an amazing organization that operates large floating hospitals. We applied to live on the *Africa Mercy*, which visits ports along the coast of Africa and performs life-saving operations for impoverished people. Volunteer missionaries live and serve on the former cruise ship. Terrell and I applied—my husband as a chaplain and me as a writer—and spent a week going through the orientation process to see if this was what God was calling our family to do. There wasn't a family cabin available and they told us it could be six months until we heard from them, so we returned home and back to square one. Weeks turned into months, and we were still waiting on the open door.

And then I got an e-mail from Maureen that simply said, "Kristen, I have searched and looked and asked many people, but I cannot find anyone who is helping pregnant girls in my country. It is a very big need. We need to pray and ask God to send someone to help."

My heart sank as I read her words. I got an uncomfortable feeling. I may have even said out loud, "Um, no, God. I can't start something." I put Google to work again and searched for someone—anyone—to help these girls. Maureen and I prayed that God would send someone. Here's a word of caution: be careful what you pray for! Although Terrell and I continued to search for open doors, praying and beseeching God to reveal His plan to us, I couldn't stop thinking about those desperate girls in Kenya.

※

Maureen was coming to the United States for the first time! We were as excited as she was with the news. She would be arriving in a month with a Student Life group, an interdenominational ministry that helps people know Christ through ministering at conferences and summer camps. Maureen's group was staying at a camp in Oklahoma, just an hour from my in-laws' farm. I had told my family so much about Maureen that when I suggested detouring our planned summer camping trip so everyone could meet her, they were excited.

I was still sharing my heart on my blog, looking for ways to make a difference. Through a friend, I met Dinah Monahan, founder of Living Hope Women's Centers, and wanted my readers to know what she was doing.

JULY 7, 2010

I can't explain it, but I know in my heart that God wants to use my blog to mobilize mothers to do good things for Him. I don't have time for a catchy logo or cute graphic—there are hungry babies in Ethiopia right now and there is a baby formula shortage.

My dot was connected with Dinah, one of America's greatest pro-life leaders. Besides setting up more than thirty maternity homes in America and her first in Africa, she is using her pro-life warehouse to ship formula into the suitcases of people traveling to Africa. It is saving the lives of precious starving babies in four of Ethiopia's orphanages, some in remote areas.

Dinah is running low on formula and that's where your dot comes in: there are hungry babies in Africa, and we can help them.

It is a fact that 30,000 (yes, you read that right: *thirty thousand*) children die *every day* from hunger and preventable disease. That number is so large it's hard to comprehend. But *your* donation will make a difference to *one*. Your gift of formula will save a life.

That day we raised more than two thousand dollars for baby formula.

A couple of days later, I actually said these words out loud to Terrell: "What do you think about us helping pregnant girls in Kenya?" The words were foreign on my tongue, but I couldn't hold them in.

"I think that's crazy."

"You mean as radical and crazy as selling all our possessions and moving onto a hospital boat with our young children?" I had him there.

He began firing hard questions at me—like how would we do this and where would we get money and are you nuts?

"We could hire Maureen," I blurted out. "When she goes back to Kenya at the end of the summer, she'll be graduating and will be looking for a job. We could open a maternity home patterned after ones here in the States. It's not a common practice in Kenya, but I've been doing some reading, and there is one in Ethiopia."

Terrell cautioned me about my enthusiasm, but he didn't commit me to a mental facility, so that was a good sign. I hit my knees and began talking to God about this crazy idea. "God, show us what to do. How do we help these girls in need?" I knew what we were considering had to be God's idea. I clung to Ephesians 3:20: "God can do anything, you know—far more than you could ever imagine or guess or request in your wildest dreams! He does it not by pushing us around but by working within us, his Spirit deeply and gently within us" (*The Message*).

I e-mailed Maureen and got straight to the point: "Would you be willing to help us help these young girls?" I hit "Send" and immediately jumped into educating myself on this global problem and possible solutions.

A few days passed, and Terrell and I were in the kitchen cooking dinner together when I heard my phone ping. An e-mail from Maureen! I read her response silently. I read it the second time aloud to my husband, and I nearly dropped the phone as the significance of her response hit me. I gasped, got pale, and gripped Terrell's arm.

Yes. Maureen said yes.

I was terrified beyond belief but relieved to have an answer.

✸

A few days later, we pulled our rented RV into the Student Life Camp in Oklahoma. We had gotten special permission from Compassion International and Student Life to spend time with Maureen. We saw each other from across the room and ran to hug one another. It was so amazing introducing her to my family; it was surreal the way my two worlds finally collided. The team was setting up for their busy week of camp. We helped Maureen put together a replica slum shanty in the foyer so students could see the type of home she grew up in.

We hung dozens of child sponsorship packets in the display, hoping that each one would be taken during the week.

Later that night, we sat around the little table in the RV and our family dreamed up Mercy House Kenya with Maureen, although it would be weeks later before we came up with the official name.

In between Maureen's e-mail

Introducing my kids to Maureen

and our RV trip, I had contacted Dinah and asked if she would help guide us through the process of establishing a maternity home in Kenya. Maureen wasn't familiar with the idea of a residential maternity home, so I explained the concept. It would be a home where the girls would live like a family and we could offer them counseling and medical care.

"I have a new friend, Dinah, who just opened a home like this in Ethiopia. I asked her if you could visit the home and train there," I explained to Maureen, who was learning the fine art of shelling sunflower seeds from Terrell while we talked.

For the next couple of days, we dreamed and tentatively planned and spoke words that excited us and made us quake with fear. But the more we talked, the more it felt like God was guiding us. We came up with an initial plan to register as a nonprofit in both countries—an overwhelming and intimidating task in itself. I would begin raising awareness and funds in the United States, and Maureen would begin researching real estate options for a residential home and staff job descriptions.

In between dreamstorming, we loved on this very special girl. It's common in Kenya for younger people to refer to people older than themselves as "Mom" and "Dad" as a way to show respect. Maureen honored us with those names, and it began to feel like she belonged to us. Our kids adored her like a big sister, and she fit right into our family like a daughter. We took her to Walmart and asked her what she needed. We longed to bless her as she had blessed us. I knew she had very few earthly possessions, so we filled the cart with shirts and jeans, a pair of shoes, her first blow-dryer (that would work with an adapter overseas), and a bottle of perfume. We had so much fun!

Maureen and I had a very simple desire: we wanted to help pregnant girls. We didn't know how we would do it, but we knew that was what we were supposed to do. Terrell and our kids were there for every conversation, interjecting their thoughts and ideas. We asked Maureen what she would be making on a teacher's salary if she had chosen that route, and I sighed in relief when I realized the small income from my blog would cover her salary. We hired Maureen to be the executive director, not knowing exactly what we were saying yes to, but we understood the magnitude of what we were considering and it scared us to death.

Several times over the course of the weekend, the audacity of this crazy idea hit us. Terrell and I would pass a knowing look over our kids' heads or he would squeeze my hand in reassurance or just whisper the name of Jesus in my ear. We wavered between extreme exhilaration and total nausea, but we simply could not deny that we felt the presence of God in our conversations and the Holy Spirit leading us.

When we hugged good-bye, we made promises to talk regularly over Skype, and this time we knew we'd see each other again. In the meantime, we had a lot of work to do. In my kitchen that day with heart pounding, I knew opening a home in Kenya to help pregnant girls was in direct response to what I had seen and experienced there. And while I still had more questions than answers, I knew our labor was birthing a God-sized dream.

❀ ❀ ❀

UNPINNED FAITH

Birthing something new is a painful, hard process, but most good things are. For us, saying yes was the first of a thousand unknown steps, but it was also one of the hardest. There's a loss of control when you lay down your will and pick up His.

Do you have a dream today? Perhaps you're wondering if it's your dream or His dream for you. Here are some characteristics of a God-sized dream:

- It will be bigger than your capability.
- It will require hard labor. Even with modern-day medicine, childbirth is risky. Similarly, birthing a dream requires hard, long work. It won't be easy.
- It will look impossible. You won't have the resources, details, or all the answers.
- There will be a big gap between your yes and the reality of your dream. That space is God-sized. If you have all the answers, resources, funding—the perfect plan—it might be your dream and not His. But when you don't know all the details or have all the answers, it gives God room to show up.
- It will require great dependence on God. If it fails, He receives glory in your failure. And if it succeeds, He gets the credit. God-sized dreams serve two purposes: they grow the dreamer and they give God glory. The dream starts with your small faith and ends with a mighty Savior.

———————— ✳ ————————

CHAPTER 7

THE YES THAT CHANGED
OUR FAMILY

❋

Why are God-sized dreams so compelling? Because we powerfully
experience God's presence in our lives through them. It's not about
destination. It's not what we will get if we complete the dream.
It's about a relationship. . . . The pursuit of any God-sized dream
is ultimately the pursuit of the One who placed it within you.
It's like a homing beacon for your heart.

HOLLEY GERTH

THE SIX OF US BALANCED an array of eighteen fifty-pound
suitcases, duffel bags, and backpacks filled with a variety of
donations from my readers and community on metal carts in
the middle of the crowded Nairobi airport in Kenya. Our little
family arrived in the dark terminal around 11 p.m. local time,
greeted by unsmiling, armed police. With the help of my mom,
who had made the trip with us, we had just endured a grueling
twenty-four hours of travel, and we were beyond exhausted.
This was our first family trip across the globe, and our three
kids were handling it like champs. That's not to say we didn't
have our fair share of THAT family moments on the plane,
such as making macaroni with a dried packet of cheese and boil-
ing water we got from a flight attendant because our youngest
refused to eat prawns, chutney, or Yorkshire pudding. I couldn't

really blame her and might have eaten the macaroni too if she would have let me. And there was the epic meltdown during the layover in London that shouldn't have surprised us. What other four-year-old can stand in yet another security line without wailing when it's really 2 a.m. her time? It was a little crazy when she insisted on taking off her clothes in aisle 32, seat D, but I can laugh about it now. What happens on the plane stays on the plane, right?

I counted bags and kids one more time and called Maureen from the airport because I didn't see her waiting for us in the baggage area as we had planned. She didn't answer the first two calls, and I began to feel panicky. When I called again, she answered breathlessly after four rings. Maureen's thick British accent makes it challenging for me to understand her on the phone. "Mom Kristen?" she said. "I am so sorry for not being at the airport to welcome you to our country."

I held a finger in my ear to drown out the background noise and said, "Where are you?"

"On the side of the road," she said. "It has been raining here, and our van slipped off the road, and we have been stuck in mud for hours." Maureen made arrangements with drivers from Compassion International to pick us up, so we continued waiting.

I was bone tired, stranded in an unknown foreign country (remember, I had been there only once before), at a crowded, intimidating airport with our children and about a thousand pounds of donated maternity clothes, baby clothes, shoes, towels, sheets, plastic dishes, and cups, and it was all I could do not to cry.

After a while, two men who spoke broken English approached

us and told us they were our drivers. We were skeptical at first, but then we heard them mention Susan from Compassion, the leader from my blogging trip the year before, and decided we were too tired to doubt. We loaded one van full of luggage and piled into the other, and we drove for what seemed like forever. My kids finally fell asleep while Terrell, my mom, and I rode in silence. The drivers didn't say a word to us. Finally, we pulled off the main road onto a dark, bumpy one where we couldn't even see our hands in front of our faces. "Where are we going?" I whispered to Terrell.

His eyes were as big as saucers. "I have no idea where we are. I've never even been on this continent." My mom grabbed my hand and said, "This is the part of the trip where the foreigners are driven down a deserted road and robbed." I laughed nervously, hoping she was joking.

Suddenly, the van stopped in what looked like the middle of nowhere and the door slid open. There stood Maureen, mud splattered across her shirt. She climbed in and rode with us the rest of the way. As I hugged her tightly, I finally could breathe easier for the first time since landing in Kenya.

❉

We arrived safely at the large, beautiful residential home our organization had rented a few months earlier less than a mile from a shopping center in town. I had only seen pictures of it, and they didn't do the compound justice when I saw it in the daylight. A lush landscape of banana and avocado trees, gorgeous tropical plants, and a vast garden covered the acre within the cinder-block walls. As we drove through the gates, we met Annette, the housemother we had only talked to over Skype, and our first three pregnant teen residents: Quinter, Charity, and Cindy. They were eerily silent, some seeing white faces for the very first time. Looking back, I'm sure that the extreme change in their living circumstances as well as meeting us was pretty overwhelming for them.

Maureen directed us to the empty beds awaiting future girls; our three kids and my mom were in one room and my husband and I next door. The electricity was out (a common occurrence we would get used to), but a single candle cast a dim light on the mosquito nets that hung over the beds. There were welcome notes on our pillows. The kids fell asleep immediately, and my mom and I covered them with a blanket. I said good night, slipped into our room, and collapsed on the firmest bed I'd ever lain on.

Even though I was exhausted, sleep eluded me for a while. There were screeching monkeys outside our open window (I thought they were dogs), but Terrell was snoring deeply. I was just about to doze off when I heard my youngest child scream. I jumped out of bed and felt my way to where she slept. She was waving her arms wildly, tangled in the mosquito net, confused and afraid. Thankfully, the rest of the family was too jet-lagged to wake up. As I tried to comfort and calm her, I prayed it would work on me, too.

I was finally back in the place that had broken my heart, and I was half-terrified, half-thrilled to be there.

✳

It had been eleven months almost to the day since we'd dreamed up Mercy House Kenya in the RV in Oklahoma with Maureen, and countless miracles had happened between that day and this one.

When we had driven the rented RV back to our home in Texas, we had spent the miles throwing out ideas about our dream. We knew God was directing us, but there was quite a gap from where we stood at point A with a general idea and point B, which represented actually opening the doors to a home in Kenya. We knew we would need a lot of money to make this happen. At the beginning, we weren't really living in a missional community that would dream with us. We had attended the same church for several years, but we struggled to engage in community and eventually looked elsewhere for it.

Over the next months, Maureen and I got comfortable with Skype, talking nearly every day for an hour or two, and I helped walk her through registering a maternity home, the first of its kind in Nairobi. Early in the process, Kimberly, a missionary mom in Kenya who happened to read my blog, e-mailed me and offered to help in any way she could. With her understanding of Kenyan law, we realized we needed to form two separate organizations, one in Kenya and one in the United States. Everything we were doing was uncharted waters for both of us, and Google became our friend.

We poured our energy and time into learning the vast world of constitutions and bylaws and board members for other nonprofits. Terrell and I didn't know any other nonprofit leaders, and navigating this complicated world was hard work. We had no idea what we were doing, so we prayed and took one step at a time. I started the paperwork to turn our idea into a registered nonprofit. All those small, unsure steps were actually adding up, and by the fall of 2011, Mercy House Kenya was an official 501(c)(3) in the United States and Rehema Rescue Centre was an official charity in Kenya (*rehema* is Swahili for mercy).

While we didn't know how we would accomplish this lofty goal of starting something from nothing, Maureen and I were compelled by one simple thought: we wanted to help pregnant girls living in extreme poverty. Our mission statement says just that: "The Mercy House exists to raise funds to provide alternative options for pregnant girls living in the streets of Kenya by aiding them in education, nutrition, housing, prenatal care, Bible study, counseling, and job skills for sustainable living."

Why Mercy House exists.
It's this simple.

This is the part of the story where God began to make it very clear that my ways are not His ways. If you had asked me how we would raise a large amount of money, I would have handed you a list of churches and people I knew who had money. We felt compelled to step out in faith and help girls in the slums, but we had more questions than answers.

I'll never forget sitting down with Terrell—our bills, monthly budget, and savings account figures in front of us—and trying to decide how far we could take this dream before it financially ruined us if no one dreamed with us. While we knew this was a journey of faith, it seemed like a daunting task, especially since we were doing it alone.

"This could ruin us, you know," Terrell said as we stared at our bank statements and 401(k) account. "I think we can do this for two years at the most."

"We will get churches and the readers of my blog to help us. They know about Maureen, and they followed my story about Africa," I tried to reassure him. But deep down, I was scared and he was too. "Let's pray." Again.

"God, You know we are terrified. But we believe You have led us to this point. We don't know how this is going to work, but we are trusting You to show us."

I spent hours lying awake at night during this season, trying to figure it out. I even jotted down a list of names of people I knew who had money. I thought we had a good plan.

We were wrong. God had better plans.

❋

Every day I wore the beautiful copper pendant Terrell had given me for Valentine's Day before I left for Kenya the first time. It was a reminder of where I'd left my heart. People constantly commented on it, remarking how unusual and pretty it was. A couple of friends who were adopting asked if me if Terrell would make them one. We thought, *Maybe we could sell these to help fund Mercy House.*

I knew I had married a very handy and creative guy, but I didn't realize the extent of his jewelry-making skills. He set up a worktable in the garage, and we found a supplier for sheets of copper, stamping tools, and colorful crystal beads. Terrell watched YouTube videos and learned how to turn a pile of beads and fine wire into a necklace. He used a scroll saw to cut the copper into the shape of Africa and then filed the edges smooth. Terrell also created round dome pendants that said "love mercy" on them. We started having beading parties with friends, family, and neighbors, and even our kids learned to string the colorful crystal beads to make beautiful necklaces. DaySpring, a company I wrote for, bought one hundred at a time to support Mercy House, and we sold hundreds of them online.

I still get emotional every time I think about the Tuesday I announced on my blog what God was birthing in our hearts. We asked families to commit to $25 a month, and in exchange they would receive a "love mercy" necklace. Robin, my faithful blog friend, responded and committed first; by the end of the day, there were a hundred more. All day long, as commitments came in, I sighed with relief. We didn't really know how much it would cost to run a maternity home in Kenya, but we were off to a good start. I called Terrell twenty times that day, between answering e-mails and sending a "love mercy" necklace to each person who partnered with us. God was building His house of mercy in the most unlikely way.

SEPTEMBER 29, 2010

I'm afraid some of you have misunderstood.

There have been words thrown at me the last couple of weeks—godly, good, brave, crazy . . .

I'm not worthy of any of them (*except maybe that last one*).

The Mercy House is a home God is building. My family is *honored* to be on the construction crew, along with our fellow laborers, Maureen and people just like you. When I look in the mirror, I don't see those words reflected. I see a scared woman who sleeps too little and worries too much. She tries to carry the weight of the world on her shoulders and has to remind herself, when the burden is too heavy, to give it back to God.

Our family isn't any different from yours. We are ordinary people. Our garbage can stinks. Our kids talk back and throw fits in open places. Our marriage is a miracle. Our dog looks longingly at her leash. We are just like you.

The other night after hammering dozens of copper pendants, my hubby said, "So this is what it feels like to jump off a cliff?"

I laughed. Then I cried. "Free-falling isn't so bad, huh?"

I was just given a glimpse into God's heart (the poor), and I couldn't turn away.

Now that I have seen . . . I am responsible. We are ordinary; *God is anything but.*

When you look into my life, if you have seen anything out of the ordinary, He gets the glory for it.

Are you standing on the edge? The first step off into the unknown is terrifying. But don't worry, He won't let you fall. *He is extraordinary.*

When we said yes, we didn't say it alone; so many others, mostly families just like ours, said yes too. I remember lying in bed with my husband that night and trying to calm the storm that was brewing in our hearts. *People trust us; this is real. What if we let them down? What if we fail?* We didn't know if we would land on our feet, but we knew we were being faithful to our God-sized dream and He was asking others to jump with us.

Our yes caused a beautiful, unexpected ripple. Countless stores donated items for us to sell, mothers signed up to be monthly sponsors, families donated supplies for when we opened our doors, connections all over the globe were made, and we found a community of people who said yes with us in our God-sized dream. It was as if people were poised all over the world, waiting for someone to say yes to starting a maternity home in impoverished

Kenya. Because the minute we responded, countless others said yes with us.

One of those moms was Suzanne Box. Her e-mail stood out in my overflowing inbox because she said she lived within an hour of me. While I didn't make a habit of meeting strangers on the Internet, Suzanne was a professional photographer and mentioned how she'd like to make my pictures more appealing (which was a kind way to say, "Don't quit your day job, Kristen, to become a photographer"). We met one weekday halfway between our two homes at a Chick-fil-A, and we began what would become one of the richest friendships in my life. Suzanne is one of those rare people who gives wholeheartedly and sacrificially, not to get anything in return but simply because she loves Jesus and believes in the work of Mercy House. She has not only provided countless beautiful photographs, she volunteers hours every week and has traveled twice with me to Kenya to help tell the amazing story of what God is doing through her gift of photography.

About the same time I got Suzanne's first e-mail, another blog reader named Lindsay e-mailed me and mentioned that her husband, Mike, was a web designer and would donate his design

Suzanne, Maureen, and me

services to help create a professional website. Terrell and I had created the first one, and it was lacking to say the least. Not only did Lindsay and Mike create a functional, professional website, they have since revamped it, provided graphics and videos, and generously supported Mercy House.

I have a picture at home to remind me of our small beginnings. Terrell is holding up a hand-drawn sketch over Skype to teach Maureen how to hook up a printer to her computer—the first piece of office equipment we purchased. Most of her life, Maureen hadn't had the luxury of electricity, so anything that had plugs was fairly new to her. There were also vast cultural differences. Some days we would spend an hour just trying to understand what the other person was saying!

One day as we were talking, Maureen's family crowded around her computer to say hello. At the time, we didn't have a rented home yet and Maureen worked from the small home she shared with her mother, siblings, and nephew. I was getting ready to send a package over to Maureen, and after greeting her family, I thought it would be fun to include a couple of bags of candy, a rare treat, in the parcel. So I asked Maureen's teenage brothers and young nephew if they liked Snickers. "Yes!" they cheered. "We would love new snickers!"

When it was just Maureen and me face to face, I mentioned how much her brothers must like candy. "Candy?" she asked, confused. I described a Snickers candy bar to her and she bent over, laughing hysterically.

"What?" I asked, confused.

"My brothers thought you said sneakers. You just agreed to send each of them a new pair of tennis shoes!" It was an expensive mistake, but picking out new shoes for her brothers and nephew is one of our family's cherished memories.

Even with the challenges of communication and the temperamental Internet, we didn't give up, and I truly believe the

Holy Spirit joined our hearts and minds for the very difficult road ahead. It wouldn't be long until Maureen would amaze us with her dedication, fortitude, integrity, and love for others as she became adept at new tasks like budgeting, accounting, and so much more.

Our vision was to develop an indigenous work that empowered Maureen—and ultimately, Kenya—to meet the needs of each girl we would help. We were partners, working together on opposite sides of the world.

❃

God taught all of us so much along the way. Because Maureen would be the one overseeing the day-to-day matters of Rehema House, we spent hours putting together a detailed operations manual for her to use (which she and her staff have revised several times since). I was so proud the day I printed out a copy, put it in a binder, and packed it up with a small video camera and a few supplies that were easier to find in the United States, like Bible study books and curriculum. I had bought a colorful dress for Maureen that matched her sassy personality, and I included a bag of Snickers and other treats for Maureen's family. I was excited to get it off in the mail; the post office clerk promised it would be there in three weeks.

It arrived nearly on time, and the Kenyan post office called to let Maureen know her package was there—her first one from the United States. But when she arrived, the clerk wouldn't give it to her unless she paid him a bribe. She couldn't believe it. She angrily refused and left empty-handed, later recounting the story to me via Skype.

The next day the post office called again about the box. She traveled by city bus to get it, and although it wasn't the same clerk, she was again asked for a bribe before he would give her the package. Again she refused. This scenario went on for days. Finally I asked her how much the bribe was. It amounted to around seventy-five US dollars.

"That's not very much. Why don't you go ahead and pay it?" I didn't think I could see her disappointment another night on Skype.

"I am a woman of God," she said. "I will have integrity, and I will not be a part of corruption."

I don't remember ever being so humbled.

"This is what we're going to do," she instructed me. "We are going to fast and pray until God releases that package to us."

And that's exactly what Maureen and I did. We prayed together over Skype and then separately over the next few days. Later that week, I heard her squeals when she opened that box.

It would be one of countless lessons that God would teach me about prayer and fasting. We faced unbelievable spiritual warfare in those first eleven months, from hiring a qualified staff to the realization that the budget we had initially set was a mere drop in the bucket, considering how expensive life was in a country that consisted of extreme poverty and extreme wealth. Just weeks before Maureen was to move into the maternity home, she tragically lost two immediate family members unexpectedly. Walking with her through the loss of her nine-year-old nephew, Demetrius, and older sister, Jacqueline, within three weeks of each other was one of the hardest experiences of my life. I was helpless. I sent her Scripture, cried with her, prayed over and for her, and we helped meet the heavy financial burden of two unexpected funerals. It was an unpleasant reminder of how hard life in poverty can be when a nine-year-old child dies from a preventable disease like tuberculosis, and his mother, in her late twenties, grieves herself to death.

But even in Maureen's deep mourning and heart-wrenching grief, she never stopped serving Jesus. She continued to take steps toward opening up Rehema House, and I learned more from her about faith and servanthood and trusting Jesus in a year than I had in my entire life going to church.

Maureen recruited and hired a qualified staff of three for the home itself, as well as additional guards. She traveled all over the city looking for a suitable location for a residential home, converted a cargo van into our future Rehema House vehicle, and began interviewing girls.

In the beginning, finding unwed pregnant girls was easy. It's a rampant problem in the slum. But convincing them to trust us was much harder. Maureen started visiting local slums and just spreading the word about the rescue center, and through word of mouth, she began connecting with possible residents. We had established a specific focus for our ministry: pregnant girls between the ages of fourteen and seventeen who had become pregnant due to circumstances beyond their control or had been seeking abortions. Orphaned or homeless girls would take priority. Most important, they had to be willing to go with Maureen of their own free will. Rehema House was looking for the most desperate. We wanted to find the worst cases, and it didn't take long before we discovered them.

In the United States, I raised funds, traveled to conferences to raise awareness of women's health issues, collected donations, and asked people to help us. Maureen and I would come together each day on Skype to share our victories and defeats, our tears and fears. We were an unlikely pair on uncharted waters, but our common goal of helping lost girls in a hopeless world united us and gave us purpose.

✳

I have to be honest. That initial year was hard, and many days the burden on our little family felt suffocating. We spent nearly every weekend in the beginning either making jewelry as a family or selling it at conferences or in our online store. Terrell taught himself how to navigate the complicated world of nonprofit bookkeeping and accounting in the cracks of his time, and we began the daunting task of recording every donation that came in. We had given people the option of different monthly donation amounts, which wasn't unusual. But I wanted to create an entry point for everyone to give something. I suggested that we include a three-dollar monthly commitment, and Terrell thought it was a great idea. Hundreds of people made that pledge, which engaged so many more people in a worthy cause and strengthened our small organization like nothing else. But it was a bookkeeping nightmare!

In the early days, I paid Madison a dime for every name she entered into the computer in an effort to keep up with the enormous workload. Still, with every passing day, our family's focus began to shift from being all about us to all about Him and others. Because record keeping was so time-consuming, it moved to the top of our prayer and priority list. We began to pray that God would provide help in this area.

A few weeks later, I got an e-mail from a grandmother who lived nearby and read my blog. She wanted to volunteer in our garage-turned-shipping-central for our online store. After one day preparing packages in our hot, humid garage, I knew it wasn't a good fit for Carol. As I thanked her and she prepared to leave, she said, "Do you happen to need any volunteers to help with data entry? It's my gift."

Tears welled up as I explained the burden our family was under to input the vast number of small donations each month. "Do you know what it's like to be someone's answer to prayer?" I said. "Because you are." From that day to this, Carol has faithfully and expertly entered thousands of donations into the Mercy House database.

Karen, another longtime friend in my community, jumped in and helped us process orders for our online store, and her family supports the organization financially. She still drops off printed orders and postage every Wednesday. We were over-whelmed, but we were not alone.

I had asked a lot from my family. They were sacrificing time and money, and I wanted them to experience it firsthand, to walk the red dirt roads with me. I wanted my children to see what I saw and fall in love with Kenya, so as we worked, we also prepared to take our first trip overseas. Instead of sharing just a Scripture and prayer at our family dinnertime, we'd join hands and ask God for the next miracle on the list.

During this first year, we failed a lot. Our kids saw us at our worst and best, stretched further than we thought possible by a dream that only grew bigger. We spent hours working instead of playing with them. We said no to family vacations and saved our money for a trip to Kenya. Mercy House turned me from a stay-at-home mom who wrote a blog part time to a full-time work-from-home mother. But I learned that if I didn't show our children the weak places and the enormous needs, they wouldn't be able to rejoice with us in the victories and miracles.

Nine months had passed since we'd said yes—the longest and shortest nine months of my life. After school one day, I gathered the kids around the computer so they could see a photograph of Quinter, our first long-awaited pregnant Rehema House resident. "Why isn't she smiling, Momma?" one asked me, looking at her sad face. My heart knotted up. *How much should I tell them about what had happened to Quinter?* Being completely open with my kids had been an ongoing internal struggle for me for the last couple of months. *How much is too much for their young minds?* I had defined some pretty horrible words to my children like *rape*, *prostitution*, and *abortion*.

"She is seven and a half months pregnant," I explained. "She has been abused and she's hungry. She will smile one day." I told them she had just had her first shower in running water, turned on her first light, and had her first doctor's visit so they could see how her baby was doing.

With a picture of Quinter's face filling the computer screen, our yes felt very real.

And worth it.

❋

Terrell flew home from a weeklong business trip the night before our family's trip to Kenya. I had packed our suitcases and a dozen bags of donations during the week, but I wasn't feeling well. As much as I didn't want to take the time, I realized it would be a good idea to get checked out before we began our long journey. It would be foolish to leave home, where medical help was readily available, with some kind of bug that might only get worse. I told Terrell I was going to the nearby urgent care center to get an antibiotic.

When the on-call doctor came into the examination room, I explained my general symptoms to him—achiness, nausea, fatigue. Since I had mentioned our trip the next day, the doctor ordered a blood draw. A short time later, he returned and said, "I'm sorry, Mrs. Welch." *Why is he apologizing to me?* I looked at him, confused.

"You won't be going to Africa tomorrow. You are in renal failure."

I was in complete shock and spent the next ten minutes arguing with the urgent care doctor. "I have to go to Africa tomorrow," I cried. After he explained to me about kidney functions and creatinine levels, he showed me the actual test results on a printout. And as if that wasn't convincing enough, he said these words: "Mrs. Welch, if you get on that plane, you could very well die in Kenya."

I called Terrell. He left a hurried message for Maureen and rushed to the hospital, leaving our sleeping children in my parents' care. The next few hours were a nightmarish blur as I was hooked up to IVs and admitted to the hospital for the next five days.

As I lay in that hospital bed, a battle was raging in me. *Why, God? Why?* I asked. *Where are You? What are You doing? What will we do? How can You allow this to happen?* God was silent. I wasn't sure if God was protecting my family from the unknown in Kenya or if Satan had derailed our plans. After five days, I was released from the hospital, but I still needed to fully recuperate before leaving the country. Thankfully, I sustained only minimal kidney damage, but the doctors never found a cause for my shocking diagnosis.

More and more I prayed, "I am not in control of any of

this, God. You are the one who is. My job is to put everything in Your hands, listen, and be obedient." When Maureen heard what had happened, she was disappointed, but even more so she was terrified I might die, just like her family members. Even though our arrival was delayed, the work of Mercy House was not. Maureen and her staff got things up and running without us, which may have been God's plan all along.

Three weeks later, I got a medical all clear from the doctors. We rebooked our tickets (thanks to travel insurance and my father) and arrived in Kenya to meet Quinter, Charity, and Cindy, the first three teenagers in our home, and offer staff training. At the time, Quinter was fifteen and Charity and Cindy were both sixteen years old.

The maternity home is really equivalent to long-term foster care in the United States. The girls are residents for as long as they need to be—each mother has a unique story, and so an individual plan is created for each one of them. It's our goal and desire for each girl to receive Christ in her life and spend a minimum of two years in transformation classes, including counseling, discipleship training, education, and learning life and job skills and how to be a mom. If a girl has a parent to return to, then we work with the family by offering parenting classes, small business training, and counseling in hopes of reintegrating the resident and her baby back into her home. Some of the girls don't have a family to return to, and they stay as long as needed, gaining independence along the way.

❋

I'll never forget our very first morning in the home. We had slept in but were awakened by the sound of beautiful singing in

Swahili. I threw on my clothes, not wanting to miss a thing, and walked downstairs to find our small staff and residents standing in a circle singing to Jesus. I cried during every song. I was overcome by what God was doing. I don't know what I had been imagining when Maureen had told me they started every day with a devotion time, but this was beautiful. It didn't take long for the rest of my family to join me, and we were in awe of

the presence of God we felt. Every single morning begins this way. After songs, Scripture is shared and testimonies are given. Every night at Rehema House ends the same way.

Giving childcare lessons using dolls

During that first trip, there weren't any babies in the house yet, but we enjoyed going to prenatal visits with the three girls and establishing relationships with nurses and the ob-gyn at the nearby private hospital that would deliver our first twelve babies, saving the lives of many of them.

The first two days my family and I unpacked and organized a thousand pounds of donations. We created a maternity and baby clothes closet, sorted by size, and divided up medical and household supplies. We spent long hours doing staff training that Terrell and I had developed, teaching the girls how to make products that we would eventually sell in our online store. Madison helped teach the girls how to make paper beads from a craft book she'd brought along, and my son even taught one of the morning devotions. My mom taught basic sewing skills.

Emerson kept us all laughing, and the rest of the time my kids played outdoors within the compound.

The kids were also an effective link to our residents. It didn't take long for them to become friends. We spent a lot of time going back and forth to the city area, buying supplies for the home. We got a push lawn mower so our day guard could also be a caretaker, and Terrell taught him how to use it. We bought paint for some of the crafts we were making and tools to do a little maintenance around the home. We prepared meals together and cleaned up together, with the help of Evans, a locally trained chef we hired to help prepare food that wouldn't make us sick. Evans continues to come offer his delicious services every time our family visits. I watched my often-picky eaters fall in love with Kenyan food. They would beg for more *chapatis*, thick tortilla-like bread, and ask for seconds on green grahams, which is like lentils, and fried cabbage.

We lived like a family. My kids got so comfortable at one point that they started arguing, as siblings do, over a frog they had found. I marched them outside to correct them, and I didn't realize the residents were listening to me from the open window.

Spending a day with all our Kenyan Compassion kids

When I came back in to resume paper-bead making, Charity said, "Mom Kristen, you discipline your children?"

"Oh yes, I do," I said, sort of embarrassed.

"But you didn't beat them," she said, confused. I realized she was trying to understand the difference between how she was disciplined and what she had just witnessed. She put her arm over the swell of her belly, and I knew she needed an answer.

"I love my kids and they need to be disciplined. But it's possible to do it in love without abusing them," I explained.

And this was one of many times when I realized these girls were watching us intently, learning how to mother, how to love, *what a family looks like.* They were especially enamored of my relationship with Terrell. They watched him tenderly open the van door for me or refill my drink. They watched him play with our kids and try to make everyone laugh.

The first time I met Ephantus, in 2010

Cindy caught me on the staircase one day, and her words touched me deeply: "I hope one day I can find a husband like Terrell." I hugged her and promised her I would pray for that.

❋

One day we took time off to visit the home of Ephantus, one of the children we sponsor through Compassion International. I had met Ephantus at his Compassion center more than a year before on a blogging trip, where we spent the day playing soccer and digging through the colorful backpack my kids had helped me pack with bubbles, coloring books, and photos of our family. But this was my first visit to his home and my family's first time to meet him. It was also their first visit to a slum.

We walked down a red-dirt road, dodging a thin, hungry-looking dog and a wayward goat eating from a pile of rotting food scraps. We stepped over trash in our path as we passed row after row of small shacks. A couple of little kids dressed in rags played in the dirt with makeshift toys of rocks and sticks as we walked by. We were surrounded by poverty so thick it overwhelmed every sense. I could hear hungry babies wailing in the distance, and no matter which way the wind blew, I couldn't escape the smell of raw sewage. Within minutes, I felt weighed down by the oppression that accompanies slum life.

I followed my friend Susan from Compassion, with my children between us and Terrell and my mom behind us. I whispered words of reassurance and encouragement to my children as they absorbed extreme poverty for the first time. I wanted them to feel safe.

We walked through a gate and ducked under worn, faded clothes hanging from a clothesline. I immediately recognized the colorful backpack drying on the clothesline and felt a wave of emotion. I pointed it out to my family excitedly, and they seemed to grasp the significance of Ephantus's precious possession drying in the sun. As we neared his home with paper-thin

Terrell and Ephantus

walls and a corrugated tin roof, Ephantus stepped out with his mother, Mary.

He was excited to see us; his grin made me temporarily forget the intense atmosphere. I hugged him. Within minutes he was holding hands with my kids and Terrell had him laughing.

"It feels like he's our brother."

After a few minutes, my little girl tugged at my arm and whispered in my ear, "It feels like he's our brother."

I whispered back, "He is." *There isn't another place in the world I'd rather be right now.*

Mary invited us into her small, tidy home, and we crowded into the room where a bedsheet separated the one family bed from the living area, which consisted of a couple of chairs. If Terrell stretched his arms out, he could touch the walls on either side of the small home. Mary welcomed us in careful English, and Susan asked her to pray. As the Swahili prayer washed over me, I bit my lip and tried not to cry. Before she said amen, I felt an animal under my legs. I gasped and then jumped up. We all laughed when a thin, scraggly cat appeared. My four-year-old was thrilled with a furry friend, and I prayed God would protect her from ringworm.

Mary began thanking us for sponsoring her son. She told us how well he was doing in school and how much he was learning at the Compassion center each week. She pointed out his newer shoes, and her bright smile lit up the dim room. As if allowing us to visit and see what our small donation did each month weren't enough, Ephantus's mother took me by the hand and half-dragged me excitedly to the edge of the road. My three children and husband followed, dodging trash and debris with every step.

I had no idea where she was taking us, but something deep within me knew this moment in my life was important.

She stopped and pointed to a broken-down shack on the other side of the road, separated by a toxic-looking green stream. I looked at her, confused. "You did this," she said in her few English words. As I looked closer, I saw bananas, limes, tomatoes, and bunches of carrots tied in small plastic bags. The shelves were lined with leather sandals, colorful handbags, paper jewelry, and bars of soap.

She jumped over the murky water and urged us to step onto the fragile-looking bridge tied together with ropes and wood. I carefully crossed with Terrell, the kids following. Just as I made it to the other side, I heard a cracking noise and turned to see my nine-year-old son's foot go through the boards on the bridge and land in the sewage water. I swallowed hard and closed my eyes. My mom immediately helped him and pulled wipes from her bag.

Mary and me

I walked up to the shelves and touched a handmade bag crocheted from plastic and looked at Mary, asking, "Did you make this?" She nodded proudly. It suddenly hit me. *This is her store, her business.*

"Is this what I think it is?" I asked Susan.

"Yes. Mary used the family gift you sent the year before to start a small business. It supports her family, helps send her children to school, and keeps them fed."

Mary had been watching me while I talked to Susan. When she saw that I understood what I was seeing, she grabbed me by the shoulders and said firmly, "You changed my life." A tear trailed down her dusty cheek.

I held on to her and a sob escaped me. The *small* gift from our family had helped her family in such a *big* way. I pulled back and looked into her eyes, my heart hammering in my chest. "No, Mary, you have changed our lives."

※

For nearly the entire three weeks we were there, Quinter never said a word, the shock of her ordeal still too raw. Charity, orphaned at a young age, struggled to get along with others

since she had been surviving on her own for so many years. Cindy was the most outgoing, her warm, loving personality winning us over the moment we met. I believe that our yearlong preparations paid off almost immediately, and I was certain that they would establish a strong foundation for the future. But as important as the practical things were, it was the presence of

Maureen and me

us as a family—a father and a mother, loving and raising their children together—that was the greatest gift we offered those three young women that first trip.

Saying good-bye was so hard. Not only had we fallen in love with our residents, we were leaving Maureen. And this time it affected all of us, not just my own heart.

Reentry back home was easier for me than before. I knew I was doing something worthwhile, and it felt good. But Terrell struggled—not only with processing his exposure to extreme poverty but also with returning to his corporate America job. He knew his hard work was providing the financial means for us to continue the work overseas, but that didn't make it any easier. Our children also struggled with processing the poverty they had seen and the new relationships they had formed. We talked a lot, cried even more, and prayed that God would help us transition back into our American lives.

Just a few weeks after we got home, I received the call we'd been waiting for—Quinter was in labor. Because of her malnourishment and lack of prenatal care before coming to Rehema House, Quinter needed to have an emergency C-section. The physician told Maureen that this girl and her baby would have died in the slum without her intervention.

Maureen received another call and brought Sarah, our fourth resident, into the home. Sarah has one of the most devastating stories of all of our girls, and just a month after entering Rehema Rescue Centre, she tried to commit suicide by drinking laundry chemicals. I got a phone call from Maureen a few months after we'd been home. We prayed hard for Sarah. She entered intense counseling, and we began to see God do a beautiful work in her heart.

Meanwhile, more babies were born. Charity gave birth to Travis, our first boy, and Cindy had Nicholas, and we continued to add more residents. Maureen and I continued to talk daily

The first eight babies born at Rehema House

about struggles with the new moms, transformations that needed to happen, how to address situations when the girls didn't get along. While babies grew, I was doing my best to raise money through writing, speaking, and hosting silent auctions on my blog; adding products like T-shirts and tote bags to the online store; traveling to conferences; and managing my own family.

The following summer we returned to hug eight mommas and eight precious babies, ranging in age from Quinter's one-year-old to our new "twin" six-week-olds born the same day to different mommas. One of the newest babies was named Maureen. This time, we couldn't keep Quinter quiet. She had transformed into a beautiful, silly girl who had a lot to say. Charity had fallen in love with her baby, against all odds, and Cindy had stepped into a strong leadership role among our newer young moms.

So much had happened since our last visit—we saw broken girls made whole by the power of God, holding babies who shouldn't be alive. Edith was our eighth resident. We had intended to stop at six, but as long as we had an empty bed and God continued to bring us hopeless, desperate girls, we continued to say yes.

Hawi is the only baby who came into our home outside of her mother's womb. A few weeks before she was born, someone had referred Edith to Maureen, but Maureen wasn't able to find her. When she finally located her, Maureen was shocked. Edith was an indentured servant and didn't even know she was pregnant until she was going into premature labor. The employer wanted nothing to do with her and allowed Maureen to take her.

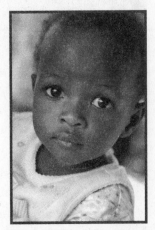

When Maureen saw the three-day-old baby, she knew something was terribly wrong. Edith didn't know how to feed her baby, so she had been dripping water from a rag into the child's mouth. Maureen took them straight to the hospi-

The eighth Rehema House baby—named after Maureen

tal, where they were both kept for weeks—Edith with a severe infection and the baby suffering from starvation and jaundice. Doctors again marveled at Maureen's timing to save these lives. Edith named her baby Hawi, which means "God's favor."

Seeing my children contentedly changing diapers and rocking babies made every sacrifice we had made as a family worth it. Our first African baby, Precious, is now nearly three years old, and her momma, Quinter, has been completely transformed into a woman of God.

✦

Back home on the second anniversary of saying yes, Terrell and I went out for an unusual celebration. We had our babysitter come at our kids' bedtime, and we went to a tattoo parlor. We had been contemplating this for many months, and when Terrell heard about a reputable place nearby, we made an

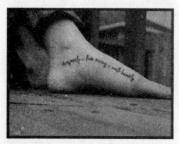

My tattoo

appointment. We wanted to commemorate our yes and the way God had branded our hearts to love mercy. From my first step on African soil, when I didn't know what I was supposed to do, God had put Micah 6:8 on my heart:

> He has shown you, O mortal, what is good.
> And what does the LORD require of you?
> To act justly and to love mercy
> and to walk humbly with your God.

I had these words etched permanently on the arch of my left foot: *Act justly. Love mercy. Walk humbly.* The same verse is on Terrell's shoulder.

How does a God-sized yes change you? This is how it changed our family and can alter yours, too.

- *We live scared.* I would be lying if I didn't admit my unspeakable fear of taking my kids into a developing nation. But once I admitted they belonged to Him (and that bad things happen in America, too), I knew it was really the loss of control that scared me because God holds their lives in His hands, I don't. And my kids? They were the least scared of us all. Not only did they trust us, they trusted God's control. Your dream should terrify you. If it doesn't, do you really need God to accomplish it?

- *We take more risks.* I married a risk-taker. He's naturally brave. I'm not. But living scared has produced a dependence on Jesus like nothing else. It also gives you the courage to do things you didn't think you could. I thought the extreme poverty we exposed our children to would wreck them like it had me. It didn't. They were resilient, with the attitude, "This is bad. How can we help?" It taught me so much about their child-like faith. Since coming home, when I have mentioned needs, they are apt to offer suggestions that make me uncomfortable. Any time there is a financial need like an unexpected, expensive van repair in Kenya or another C-section, they remind me of what God has already provided. They trust what they can't see because God has been faithful.

- *We depend on God more.* We've asked God for some pretty big things—huge financial provision, supernatural healing in our girls, wisdom and direction, and so much more. Sometimes I'm the first to forget His provision when a new request presents itself. My kids often remind me of what God has done. They simply believe.

- *We see more miracles.* Because we've made it a habit to share the needs with our kids, they have also seen the miracles. From God stretching food to feed seven hundred hungry kids in the slum to a raped momma falling in love with her baby, we have the privilege of not only asking for the impossible but also seeing it come to pass.

So when one of my children is worried about a big math test coming up, she doesn't hesitate to take her concern to God.

- *We are more generous.* Maybe it's because we've seen God provide so much from such unlikely sources, but this whole process has made us more generous. Just down the street from our home, we saw a needy family on the corner holding up a sign, asking for food. When my kids asked if we could help, I couldn't say no. I pulled up to the nearby ATM, and when they suggested I withdraw five times the amount I was planning, it humbled me. They understand how much we've been given, and they are generous because of it!

- *We lost and we gained more than we thought we would.* While this amazing God-story is beautiful, it has also been painful and lonely at times. We have lost friends along the way, some who said the choices we've made make them feel uncomfortable. My kids clearly are traveling on the "narrow road" and are aware how few find it; they can tell you why it's so important that we live for Jesus and not for others. Even though we've lost some friends, we've also gained others. We've found joy communing with like-minded believers during this journey.

- *We have perspective.* When the kids held those babies on our last trip to Kenya, I knew they recognized where our treasure was being placed. Even though our visits are relatively short, our kids' perspectives have been broadened. They return home to their American culture, knowing how the rest of the world lives.

●◉●

UNPINNED FAITH

I knew saying yes to something so much bigger than our family would be challenging and life changing. There were times it was downright scary and it didn't feel safe. Saying yes will cost you something. It will challenge and stretch you.

Our yes altered our future because the dream has deeply changed how we live out our faith. Hebrews 11:6 says, "Without faith it is impossible to please Him, for he who comes to God must believe that He is, and that He is a rewarder of those who diligently seek Him" (NKJV).

- Is God asking you to say yes?
- What is holding you back?
- Take a minute and ask Him what He is speaking to you about today.
- What first small step are you willing to take in faith to realize that dream?

———— ✱ ————

CHAPTER 8

THAT MESSY PEACH PIE

———— ✳ ————

Do you know that nothing you do in this life will ever matter,
unless it is about loving God and loving the people He has made?
FRANCIS CHAN

I COULDN'T BELIEVE IT. Here we were, not even home two weeks from our first family trip to Kenya, and my kids had the audacity to complain because I asked them to *share their candy with each other.*

And so I went there. "How can you complain about sharing something so insignificant when you stood in a shack the size of my closet that was shared by six people? I thought going to Africa would show you how much we have. I thought it would change you!" I watched Jon-Avery's face fall and Madison's eyes fill, but I was too wrapped up in myself to respond as I stormed off, muttering about my ungrateful kids.

We had taken them on this amazing journey for many reasons, but I'd be lying if I didn't admit that I hoped it would produce more thankfulness in them. Don't get me wrong, I have good kids. No, great kids. But they are human . . . a lot like their mom; we can all stand to complain less and be more thankful.

After I cooled off, my daughter found me. "Mom, you're right, we can share. I'm sorry."

Triumph.

But she wasn't done. "Mom, Africa did change me. I feel angry at what I saw. I *am* different. I'm trying to figure all this out, but I'm still an American kid. I don't live in Africa. But I will never be the same because of what I experienced. I'm still trying to figure out what God wants me to do about what I saw and experienced. Please don't say that it didn't change me."

It was time for my face to fall. I knew that I had deeply hurt my kids with my words. I was doing the very thing I condemned them for: complaining. Later, I shared my frustration with a good friend, someone who knows me well and loves my kids dearly.

"Kristen, you're seeing your kids up close, all the time. Step back. Look at them. They are world changers. They love the lost and poor and put others first. Your kids are amazing."

She was right. It broke my heart that I couldn't see it for myself. Later that day, I apologized to them and asked for forgiveness. "Madison and Jon-Avery, I'm sorry. I am so proud of you and how you handled our trip to Kenya. You served every day, you helped with your little sister, you encouraged the staff, you spent time with the mommas-to-be. You 'loved mercy' well. I'm sorry for being so hard on y'all. Will you forgive me?"

They did, and I did what I should have done in the first place: I let them feel and process in their own way. Every trip to Kenya leaves us reeling, trying to fit what we know into what we've seen. It's a process and we haven't figured it out completely, but I'm confident we are raising truly great kids who are already successful.

And that's when I realized we were in the process of redefining success for our family. We were bucking against the world, which says success is how popular you are or how much money you make. Ever since we went to Africa, we see through a global lens, and it has deeply altered our view. Following this God-sized dream has reshaped us. Our goal isn't a fat 401(k) so we can live comfortably for ourselves; our kids aren't on the path that many of their peers are on, vying for popularity and more stuff.

That's not to say my kids don't want to be popular or have more stuff; they are kids, after all. They just recognize there's more to life. They have seen how the rest of the world lives, and they get it. They aren't weird or misfits, and they've been able to find small pockets of community in their public schools and at church. But they are known as Christians. They attend school Bible clubs before school led by Christian teachers and invite friends to church. They talk about their trips to Kenya and share their world perspective. It's not easy. It's hard when your normal *isn't normal.*

It's even harder when you're a kid and society demands that the number one goal is to fit in—and you don't. Madison explains it this way: "I love the latest fashions and having fun with my friends. I don't have social media accounts or boyfriends like most of the kids at my school, but I don't want to be like everyone else. Sure, I'm different from a lot of kids, but I feel respected for living my life this way."

Success in God's upside-down economy is supposed to look different. It's becoming less so He can be more. It's putting yourself second, others first. It's letting your kids ask hard questions and letting them teach you about true greatness. Jon-Avery asked me one night why some of his Christian friends were allowed to play teen-rated video games. I explained that parents and kids have to make their own decisions, and I asked him if we should reconsider letting him play older games.

"No, Mom. I'm glad you don't let me. I don't want that stuff in my mind," he said.

Yet we are still a very human, typical family. There's about as much dysfunction in my family as there probably is in yours. We have arguments and dirty rooms and piles of laundry. Some days I mop the entire floor with a wet paper towel because I don't want to do it for real. We take vacations and attend after-school events and have meltdowns in the toy aisle at Target too.

This journey has taught me so much about my family. How we are like a team, pitching in our strength when others are weak, making hard choices and standing together no matter what. The rest of the time we're being goofy and relaxed, passionately debating the color of the sky and picking on each other. As blogger Robert Brault has said, "Family life is a bit like a runny peach pie—not perfect but who's complaining?"[1] I think what we have as a family is deliciously healthy even though there are times when we definitely don't have it all together.

I hope you can take heart in that. I think sometimes we like to tell ourselves when we see a family serving or doing something bigger than they are that they are better than we are, that there is no way to catch up with what they have accomplished. Let me dispel the myth that doing something big for God happens only when we reach a certain stage or have moved past particularly trying phases. That's not the way it works.

God wants us right in the middle of our mess because it's the perfect place for Him to shine through our imperfections. When Adam and Eve—the first family—disobeyed and believed the lie that God didn't love them, God's perfect creation started to unravel from sin. But God went on to use people like them to be part of the love story that culminated with a baby named Jesus who rescued and redeemed God's children.

Since the family is God's means of telling His story, our goal is to build a strong family. One key aspect is having respect for each other. It doesn't say much about me if I excel at loving others (locally or globally) yet I'm mad at my daughter for losing my favorite earrings and verbally abuse her. Romans 12:10 says, "Love each other with genuine affection, and take delight in honoring each other" (NLT). Our preference is to show appreciation for each other on a regular basis.

Sometimes at our house I still hear, "You are the meanest mom!" I used to cringe when my kids said this. Now I just nod my head and remind myself that I must be doing something right. And you probably are too. But the world won't always see it that way.

I try to say yes when I can, but let's be honest—sometimes the answer needs to be no. Unfortunately, this isn't popular in our world. We live in a culture that thinks it's more important to be a yes parent—to make sure kids are happy all the time, beginning with iPads at age three, cell phones at seven, an extracurricular activity almost every night at eight, $150 shoes at nine, unlimited freedom at eleven, and dating privileges at twelve.

I'm sure some people will never see me as a good parent.

Saying yes is a whole lot easier than saying no. *No* takes courage and strength (especially if God has blessed you with strong-willed children like mine). Whenever my kids disobey, show major disrespect, or start putting on an attitude of entitlement, I send them out to the yard. We have tall, ugly weeds in the mulched areas of our front and back yards. *Y'all, we've gone months and months without a single weed.*

In an effort to raise a strong family that can withstand the shifting cultural storms that blow our way, Terrell and I are committed to raising our kids counterculturally. We take these words of pastor Francis Chan to heart: "Something is wrong when our lives make sense to unbelievers."[2] We are trying our best to build a strong family by being consistent, offering grace and understanding along the way.

And we manage to mess up every day. I lose it over Madison's room. I'm a neat freak (my kids call me obsessive about a clean house). Madison is a musician and a deep thinker. Her canvas is often her room. I have yelled and screamed and regretted making her bedroom a battleground. We finally compromised at letting her live freely in her space during the week and cleaning up her array of clothes and hangers and shoes on the weekends.

If you visited our house, you'd hear us before you saw us. We are loud and passionate. We laugh, we cry, we argue. We sing off-key, we dance in the kitchen, we complain when we shouldn't. Madison mothers Jon-Avery, telling him what to do. Jon-Avery does the same to Emerson, and Emerson takes it out on the pets.

Before you feel sorry for my kids, you should know we also provide them with love and affection; we meet every one of their physical needs and many, many of their wants. We splurge occasionally (which I think is absolutely necessary), and we invite our kids to talk to us about anything, as long as they can do it respectfully. When our kids were younger, we had "What's Your Beef?" nights every once in a while. It was a time for our kids to share their frustrations with Terrell and me.

I remember my kids telling me that they needed a space to be messy without having to pick things up the minute they were untidy, and they really felt like they needed an allowance. These nights established a good routine for my kids to talk openly and honestly with us. Of course, we don't always discuss things with the right attitude or tone, and we have hurt each other with our words, like most families. But we keep trying.

I know there are many families on the same path with us, and I hope we can encourage each other. Choosing to live counterculturally isn't easy. You will be misunderstood, even pitied. You won't fit in and neither will your kids. Your children probably will resist in some areas. Nothing is harder for kids. It means your kids won't be like everyone else. Most days my kids are okay with this, but some days it's hard for all of us. We continually teach them to trust us as we try to follow God, but we know there are some things they will never understand or like. Which brings me back to being the meanest parents ever. And honestly, I'm okay with that.

Here are twelve areas we are focusing on as a family to live counterculturally:

1. We have a family mission statement.
2. We resist spending money we don't have. Kids watch you even if you don't realize it. We try to be an example of someone who has good spending habits.

And if we should overspend, it's important to attack the debt immediately because debt becomes an encumbrance.

3. We tell our kids no if what they are asking for or wanting to do isn't right for our family. We strive to be intentional with our choices.

4. We expect our kids to work. Hard work creates a sense of pride and ownership. It encourages kids to work for what they want. We don't just buy them everything. We keep a job jar in the kitchen and reward their effort.

5. We differentiate between needs and wants. There's a lot of pressure as parents to give our kids the best of everything, but it's important to determine what they really need. We try never to skimp on what God says they need—unconditional love and grace. We make it our goal to laugh every day and be grateful.

6. We make family meals a priority.

7. We don't overschedule our kids. It's not uncommon to hear moms in my community talk about shuttling their kids around for hours every day after school. I think kids need unscheduled time at home. We limit activities outside the home.

8. We encourage alternative choices to what others are doing, challenging our kids to creatively express themselves and think outside of the box. One example I've heard of that I loved was a group of kids giving the $100 to charity that they would have spent on a homecoming football mum. They let everyone know by wearing T-shirts that said so. There's nothing wrong

with a mum or splurging for a special occasion, but the average family spends a thousand dollars on the prom. I think money can be spent more wisely.

9. We limit screen time (video games, computer, and TV). There are different ways to do this: You can set a certain time limit for each day, make it weekends only, or have a "no technology day" once or twice a week— whatever works for you. At our house, we limit the kids to thirty minutes of individual screen time a day. We try hard to enforce this during school and are more lenient in the summer. Last year, we started screen-free Sundays. When we told our kids, they flipped out. Their reaction reinforced exactly why we needed to do it. The key is consistency. Before long, we noticed our kids expected it. But we aren't legalistic about it. Some of our best memories are made when we break our own rules, pile on our bed, and watch a movie together on a Sunday afternoon.

10. We expect more from our kids than culture demands. Society says kids need stuff and all teens are lazy. We read the book *Do Hard Things* as a family. The authors, Alex and Brett Harris, challenge kids to live above what the world expects of them.

11. We allow our kids to make their own mistakes and to see ours. We don't fix everything. It's important to teach children responsibility by letting them fail sometimes. If we always rush to bail them out of problems and mistakes, they will continue to make them.

12. We splurge. It's fun to surprise the kids every once in a while by breaking one of the rules.

Disclaimer: I am the first to admit that we struggle with this list. One or more of the rules might be easy to keep consistently, whereas others are difficult. We can't be put on a pedestal for being a model family. Our main goal is to keep our focus on God and Him alone. Even with our shortcomings, I know that it's important for us to persevere. If Satan can convince us that we aren't good enough as a family to leave a positive imprint on this world, then he wins. We can't let that happen.

Because when it's all said and done, I want what we succeed at to matter for eternity. Tim Kizziar said it well: "Our greatest fear . . . should not be of failure but of succeeding at things in life that don't really matter."[3]

If these twelve rules seem overwhelming to you, start with a few and add to the list over time. I recommend two to begin with: crafting a family mission statement and gathering for a family meal each day.

CREATE A FAMILY MISSION STATEMENT

When we wrote a family mission statement in 2008, it felt bold. I had been blogging about a year, and I knew our family needed goals, something to work toward together. Our kids were all under eight years old and it seemed like a good time to teach them about intentional living.

We started by brainstorming about some goals we wanted to accomplish as a family. We talked about going on a family mission trip instead of a regular vacation and making a point to have fun on a regular basis. My kids threw the word *adoption* in there, too, and we suggested they pray for Mommy and Daddy. We talked about the two important things we knew

God wanted us to do: love Him and others, based on Jesus' greatest command reflected throughout the New Testament.

> The most important commandment is this: . . . "You must love the LORD your God with all your heart, all your soul, all your mind, and all your strength." The second is equally important: "Love your neighbor as yourself." No other commandment is greater than these. MARK 12:29-31, NLT

Here's the mission statement we came up with in 2008:

> To make a difference in the world, a single light, shining brightly in such a way that we keep Jesus our focus, listen closely to His voice, and enjoy life. So that we can say at the end of the day, we've touched others and thrived.

Two years later, I made my first trip to Kenya. We had no idea when we wrote that statement, framed it, and hung it on the wall that we would found a nonprofit to help people on the other side of the world. It's amazing (and no coincidence) that what we are doing now fulfills our mission statement in every way.

Our family mission statement

I honestly believe that writing down our mission statement set our hearts and lives in motion to say yes to the next steps as they came. Last year, I found an old wooden pallet and my kids helped me stencil the mission statement on it in bright colors. It hangs over our mantel as a clear directive for our family.

If I've learned anything in this life, it's that life is going to happen whether or not we are intentional. It's better to lead your life rather than let it lead you. When we were beginning to think about drafting our family mission statement, we looked for ideas at Families with Purpose, a company that helps parents create meaningful families. They confirmed that a family mission statement

helps create meaningful family goals
helps your family make big decisions
helps your family regain their focus
helps your family remember their passion[4]

Ultimately, a family mission statement asks this important question: *Why are we doing this?* Often when we ask ourselves why we're working ourselves sick or why we are missing dinner for nightly football practice, we discover that we are doing it because that's what everyone else is doing. That's never the right answer for any family. That's not to say that we can't work long hours or enjoy extracurricular activities, but there must be a balance of priorities. Goals are different from a mission statement. Goals are things you want to do, to accomplish. Mission statements are the whys behind what you do. Creating a family mission statement will help focus your family on what you're trying to accomplish and remind you that what you do needs to have a purpose.

GUARD THE MOST IMPORTANT MEAL OF THE DAY

There is an hour in my day that I protect fiercely. I hold off the undeniable force that tries to threaten this time—when my family gathers around the table for dinner.

I fight for dinner.

Even when there are fights at dinner.

A couple of years ago, I downloaded a great little family Lent devotional guide and envisioned healthy spiritual discussions around the table with my husband and children as we prepared our hearts for Easter.

Um, so about that.

Life happened and there were interruptions and we got nine days behind, and the last time I opened it, one of my kids was under the table having a meltdown because two of her veggies were touching something else on her plate.

In a very grown-up way, I slammed down my Kindle and said, "Just forget it." Because sometimes I forget the reason behind my intentions. I work to create an atmosphere of holiness and happiness in our home, and then humanity gets in the way or veggies touch.

We did the dishes, and as I huffed and puffed my way through them, I heard a whisper from the risen one who *is* Easter. "Kristen, I love you for who you are and not what you do."

That's what dinner is about too. It's not about the food, which I'm grateful for because sometimes my culinary creations are good, sometimes not so much. (You can have tacos—our favorite family meal—only so many nights in a week.) It's not about perfection or even fulfilling a carefully laid plan. Dinner is about the conversation, the laughter, *the being together*. It's about unplugging and connecting.

As my kids get older, I have noticed a stronger pull away from this family time. There may be playdates waiting at the door, sport practices, meetings at work and school, but I fight them all. Even though I occasionally lose the battle and dinner is a mismatched, haphazard attempt with a traveling husband or a dash out the door to a meeting, I won't give in to this battle.

Studies like one conducted by the University of Florida have discovered positive things about families that eat dinner together:

Kids are less likely to use drugs.
Families are noted as happier.
Kids have better grades.
Couples enjoy stronger marriages.
Kids adjust better to life in general.
Families produce healthier kids with better eating habits.[5]

And when teenagers were polled about the importance of regular family meals, an overwhelming majority craved family mealtime together more often. So basically, it's healthy in every way for your family.

I like to keep my family around the table for as long as possible, and some nights long is twenty minutes—total. I've found some practical ways that help us connect around the table:

- *Highs and Lows.* Go around the table and let each person say his or her high or low of the day. (This often proves to be a hilarious time together for our family. Like the time when our youngest, who was in kindergarten at the time, said, "My low was when a classmate pooped on the playground," to which my oldest piped up, "Now I have a new low." Classy, I know.)

- *Pray.* Even if it's just a quick dinner prayer, this is a perfect opportunity to connect spiritually. We usually ask who wants to pray; we mention pressing needs or burdens or pick a country to pray for. We keep a basket near the table with Bibles, books, pens, and a gratitude journal. Often what we have prayed for ends up later being a praise, so if we write it down, we can look back at what God has answered.

- *Read.* Some days dinner is our only undistracted opportunity for all five of us to be together. For years now, we've taken the time to read together around the table before we clean up the kitchen. Some months, we will read a book of the Bible verse by verse (and some nights, we get through *one* verse). We often choose a book to read a page or two from each night. I love this time together, and even though it seems slow going at times, it is worth it when we finish!

- *Draw.* There is a seven-year age gap between Emerson and her big sister, Madison. It's not always easy to find age-appropriate reading or even prayer requests that everyone is interested in. Several years ago, I primed and painted the top of our table with chalkboard paint. Once the table is cleared, anyone can have a piece of chalk. The table becomes a place to sit, talk, and doodle. I keep touching it up because it has kept us together and been a nice diversion for short attention spans.

So no more excuses! (I don't like to cook, there are practices and busy schedules, etc.) Change it. Make dinner a priority. Be creative to get that hour together because, really, we're talking about a lot more than food on a table.

UNPINNED FAITH

Are you ready to reclaim your family from the world? I suggest that you begin with two foundational things: a family mission statement and family dinners. Both are strong methods to unite your family. For us, writing a family mission statement defined who we were and who we wanted to be. It is a constant reminder that we are here on earth to serve God and reflect His love to others.

If you don't have a clue how to create a family mission statement, Families with Purpose suggests this helpful formula as a starting point:

- To . . . (do something)
- In such a way that . . . (quality of action)
- So that . . . (we gain these results or benefits)

What about family dinners? Are you ready to make them a high priority at your house? What do you need to change to make that happen?

Start today to

- Slow down and look intentionally at your calendar to see where any conflicts are.
- Have a family meeting and ask questions: Why is it important for us to do this? What school or other activity

seems more important to you? When was the last time we ate together as a family? Do we eat dinner together at least four nights a week? How can we keep our family together in the kitchen longer?

No two families will have the same answers or solutions. Each dinnertime will be as unique as the people who are participating. The important thing is to commit to making it happen.

CHAPTER 9

I'M NOT GOING TO LIE— DOING GOOD IS HARD

---❈---

Radical obedience to Christ is not easy. . . . It's not comfort, not health,
not wealth, and not prosperity in this world. Radical obedience to
Christ risks losing all these things. But in the end, such risk finds its
reward in Christ. And he is more than enough for us.

DAVID PLATT

IT WAS THE NIGHT before my fourth trip to Kenya in the spring of 2013. My bags were packed, piled by the door, my passport and itinerary tucked in my backpack. It was my first time back to Kenya without my family, and inside I was trembling.

As I went over the kids' schedule with Terrell, I stopped and closed my eyes, and with a shaky voice I said what my heart couldn't hold any longer: "Will this ever get easier? In five years will it still be this hard to go there, or even to stay here and do this work? Will my heart always be only half-willing to follow God?"

And then I cried because my own words were hard to hear.

Because, y'all, I'm still just that girl wearing that rhinestone Jesus pin. I still struggle with the same fear and doubt, the same inadequacy and uncertainty, the same desire to stay instead of go.

I carry anxiety pills for traveling and struggle with side effects from antimalarial medicine. I miss my family with every breath, and sometimes I'm so scared I can't stop shaking inside. Tears fall at the most inopportune times, and insomnia is my bed companion. It's been years since I responded yes to God, and I still feel unqualified and overwhelmed at the task.

Terrell said something I didn't expect: "Last night, I felt the same way." He was in the middle of gathering tax info for our nonprofit accountant, being stretched paper thin, frustrated with computer issues, overwhelmed with the heaviness of his full-time job, and trying to stuff more work into the few minutes of time he had in a day. "I want to help rescue girls, I want babies to be born, I want that good part—but not really the rest."

His words, although raw, comforted me because I want the good part too. I want the happy, healthy babies, the beautiful transformed girls. Don't we all? But as we've counted the cost these past few years, we have learned the good part doesn't happen without the hard.

As my husband held me and we said our good-byes, I whispered, "I just wish I was braver."

"Maybe that's why God called us. Because we aren't brave. But He is everything we're not and everything we need," Terrell said.

If I have learned anything in this journey, it's this: the good makes the hard worth it. But getting to the good part requires making it through the valley of the hard.

I'm good at organizing my family, carpool pickup, making dinner (well, sort of). I'm good at mothering (most days) and encouraging moms with my words, but living this God-sized dream continually stretches me further than I think possible. It's uncomfortable.

✳

Kenya was feeling more and more like home on this trip. I recognized the roads and shops, was able to convert dollars to shillings without blinking, could understand the unique culture and barter with the best of them. Still, during that week there, I had a panic attack every night. A full-blown freak-out session with me huddled in the corner of my bed enveloped by a mosquito net, panting and heart pounding in the dark room. I prayed and cried and begged Jesus to be near and for my anxiety medicine to kick in.

God wanted me desperate. He wanted me depending on Him, not only for direction, wisdom, and protection, but for every breath I took. Because really I am. But there's something powerful in realizing and acknowledging complete dependence on Him. I was afraid to do anything but call out to Jesus in my weakness. Jesus keeps asking me to have faith for the impossible. And it makes me desperate and I feel like I can't stand, so I have no choice but to fall on Him. He meets me there, every time.

I can honestly say that nothing about chasing this God-sized dream has been easy. Encouraging, huh? Every single step has had its challenges. Whenever I'm down in the dumps and whining about the obstacles, I'm almost always reminded that if it were easy, I wouldn't need God. This work wouldn't be miraculous and dependent on God if I had all the answers. If I made it happen nice and neatly, I would get the glory, not Him. So I am stretched and pulled and asked to believe for things that are impossible and improbable. Not only does He provide for the home He is building, He changes me in the process.

My faith has increased and I am slowly growing into this

dream. Not so I get comfortable but so that I can dream bigger, which makes me really uncomfortable. I get random e-mails from people (I'm looking at you, Terrell) that say, "Hey, what do you think about Mercy House Tanzania?" and there's a link to an article about the high rate of death among pregnant woman. I pray for the need and delete the e-mails. I haven't been stretched that far yet.

Doing good work for Jesus isn't easy. It's just plain hard. This journey has taught me a few things:

NOT EVERYONE WILL BE A FAN OF YOUR DREAM

Dreaming big has been the hardest job of my life. It has made me radical in the eyes of many people. Perhaps one of the hardest seasons in this journey was discovering that some people wouldn't dream with me. I lost friends or maybe just realized I never really had them. It's painful when someone looks at you and says, "When I look at you now, I think about poor people, and that makes me uncomfortable." You and me both. Not everyone is going to herald your dream. Your pursuit of God will make some feel awkward around you.

Let's be honest: it's hard to swallow the fact that some people won't believe in you or what you're doing. But that doesn't mean you shouldn't do it. It just means you've got to remember who you're doing it for. Think about the examples in the Bible and know that we're in good company. Jesus certainly wasn't accepted in His hometown.

But just as some distanced themselves from us, others drew near. I love how God can turn the thing that hurts you into the thing that heals you. He can take community-inflicted wounds and mature you, make you dependent on Him, and allow the body of Christ to play a big role in your healing.

DOING GOOD DOESN'T MEAN BAD DOESN'T HAPPEN

Terrell and I serve on the board of a local nonprofit that does incredible work in closed Russian-speaking countries by using sports as an open door to spread the gospel. One night in particular, we were so tired from working our regular jobs, the last thing we wanted to do was load up the family and head to a board meeting. But we had made a commitment, and we also had a personal offering we wanted to share with our friends, a blessing from a bonus my husband had gotten. Plus, we dig Russian food.

The Russian culture is built on relationship and fellowship, and I knew it would be a good but long evening. While our children played in the background, we discussed matters at hand, and as the clock moved toward my children's bedtimes, I excused myself so I could get my kids in bed early, mentally congratulating myself for the foresight of driving two cars.

Once I was home and had the kids in bed, I got an urgent call from Terrell. Apparently, Madison had borrowed his car keys to get her homework and had slipped the keys into my purse instead of his pocket. Basically, it was after 10 p.m. and he was stuck. Our kind Russian friends offered to let my husband drive their car to our house so he could retrieve his keys without pulling my exhausted children out of bed. Perfect plan.

Except that on the way home, my husband misjudged a curb and wrecked their car. He was able to complete his errand, but this was going to be an expensive night. Talk about a bad day.

To make a long story short, it ended up costing us a lot of money to attend that board meeting. I might have even asked my husband if they could apply our donation to the car repair. I'm kidding, sort of. But seriously, I was momentarily irritated with God. "C'mon! We are serving You and doing good. How can You let something like this happen?" Then He brought Romans 8:28 to my mind: He has promised to work things out for our good according to His purposes; there's nothing about promising us that there won't be some bad days in the process. "I get it, God." In light of what I've seen globally, this was definitely just an inconvenience to our pocketbook. It was a good lesson in life. The bad in our lives gives God ample room to show up and prove His goodness. He doesn't promise we won't have hardships; He promises us we won't be alone in them.

SOME STRUGGLES INTENSIFY WITH YOUR DREAM

I'm not the kind of person to see a demon around every corner or make things more spiritual than they are. But I have always believed Ephesians 6:12 to be true: "We are not fighting against flesh-and-blood enemies, but against evil rulers and authorities of the unseen world, against mighty powers in this dark world, and against evil spirits in the heavenly places" (NLT).

There has definitely been a battle going on behind the scenes in the work of Mercy House, and it's spilled over into our lives. In the first year, it seemed like every day was wrought with struggle. From forming a nonprofit to purchasing a vehicle, to fund-raising and hiring qualified staff in Kenya, we faced opposition. Not only was there a huge cultural learning curve, there was a fight for freedom and healing for our girls and the very lives of their unborn children. To put it bluntly, Satan hates God's work. He will work against you.

Every time we enter enemy ground and attempt to rescue a new girl, the battle rages. The vehicle breaks down (this has happened countless times), the girl runs away, an aunt shows up using voodoo, a neighbor tries to convince the scared girl we want to steal her baby, just to name a few. Maureen and I have also faced physical ailments; we've had sick family members and even had loved ones die.

But God has never once abandoned us. When some struggles intensify with our dream, God's presence and heavenly force intensify too. He is powerful. He doesn't let weapons formed against us prosper. He is the dream giver, and He is in control. Greater is He that is in me than he that is in the world (see 1 John 4:4). Satan will give you a rousing fight, but in the end, he will not win.

GOD DOESN'T ALWAYS CALL US TO BE SAFE

I was making a home visit on that fourth trip to Kenya, visiting the family of Cindy, one of our first rescued girls. She was blessed with a loving mother and siblings, and unlike many of our girls, she had a support system to return to after her graduation from Rehema House. The challenge was her drunk, violent father who terrorized the family. Neighbors had recently beaten him on his last drunken binge. We were hopeful he would stay away while we visited.

We filled our van with friends of the maternity home, men who could help keep us safe if the father was around. As we drove into her slum and turned down the narrow street, driving slowly through muddy potholes, there he stood. He slapped the side of the van and we ducked, hoping he was too drunk to recognize us.

The meeting inside Cindy's home

We left a couple of men in the van parked in front of the one-room home and quickly met to form a plan of action to help this family, a plan which in turn continues to help Cindy.

I silently prayed and quaked. Not only am I not brave, I love safety. I don't like taking risks or putting myself in harm's way. I'm a chicken. If you watch home videos of me as a young mother with my toddlers, I repeat, "Be careful" about 4,832 times. Safety is sort of my thing.

But there comes a moment when you either trust God or you don't and when your purpose overrides your caution. This was a moment for me when I realized and remembered who holds my life in His hands. We completed our home visit without any trouble from Cindy's dad, and we were eventually able to help temporarily relocate her family to a safer area, away from his influence.

STRIKING A BALANCE IS TRICKY

My laundry is never done. As a matter of fact, I've been known to "fluff" a load four times because I'm not quite ready to fold it. My counters are sticky, and some weeks the only times I go upstairs to my kids' rooms are to tuck them in. I try not to look to the left or right, and there is some deep-breath-taking as I step over their piles. Messes make me feel out of control.

I love my home and the people who live with me. Without a doubt, they are my ministry. I can try to create an amazing career or impact the world with a global nonprofit, but if I end up with a family who is ignored or resentful of my efforts, what have I gained? More than anything, I want to work alongside my husband and children because it's in serving together that we are all changed. My burden becomes their burden. My heart for those in need becomes their hearts. But this is only accomplished through love for each other.

I've noticed that when I get that "everything is out of control" feeling, I tend to panic and become a control freak. I take it out on my floors and the dirt in my house and, most often, my family. And I'll just add, working in a third-world country, I sometimes feel that everything is out of control all the time. If I'm not careful, my little family gets the brunt of something I could never control.

But here's the deal: when God is in it, He doesn't need us to control a thing. As a matter of fact, the only way we can truly make a difference is by releasing control to Him. Ultimately, I have to rely on this truth that Chuck Swindoll phrased beautifully: "Nothing under God's control is ever out of control."

GOD KEEPS WRECKING ME

We left Cindy's house and drove over an hour down dusty, bumpy roads to the home of Elizabeth, another of our residents at Rehema House. It was her first trip back to the spot where she'd been attacked and then rescued by God and Maureen. It had been fifteen months nearly to the day. She returned for the visit with her chubby, happy baby on her hip.

I've seen a lot of poverty. But when it's personal, it wrecks you in a new way. This visit was personal. I knew this girl well; we had fasted and prayed for her healing and loved her to wholeness, believing God for transformation, and had helped her become a momma. Nine months before when I'd visited Kenya, I had literally begged her to stay in our home when she wanted to leave after her first challenging months in our care. I was invested in this precious life.

Standing in her dirt-floor home without a roof and smelling human waste from a nearby hole in the ground was personal. Sitting on the only piece of furniture in the house, a simple chair that had recently replaced a rock, while her mother thanked me for doing good, wrecked me.

I need to be wrecked. Good work is hard. Hardness dulls us and becomes our norm until we get perspective. I don't ever want to be okay with what I saw that day. I'd rather stay wrecked than satisfied with the American dream and pretending this type of poverty doesn't exist.

GOD WANTS A PURE HEART

Our desire to touch others must come from the transforming power of Christ within. Our ultimate goal should be to make His glory known. There are a lot of do-gooders in the world. A few are misguided people looking for significance. We cannot offer eternal change on our own. It is found in discovering

Christ's purpose for our lives, whether big or small, and allowing Him to use us in a way that brings recognition to His name, not our own. When His significance is seen in our insignificance, then we can know we are making a true difference. It's so much more than following through on our best intentions. As Mark Galli observes,

> The search for significance, especially if it requires changing the world, can blind us to the everyday tasks, the mundane duties, and the dirty work that is part and parcel of the life of discipleship. . . . We should honor any generation that strives for significance, especially if it is a longing to make a difference in the world. Better this than striving to make money and live a comfortable life! But the human heart is desperately wicked and the human soul subject to self-deception, and this colors even our highest aspirations. Even the best of intentions mask the mysterious darkness within, which is why we need to be healed also of our best intentions.[1]

We aren't promised comfort, fortune, or success in this life. But we are guaranteed trials and tribulations and an ultimate reward of eternity with Jesus. Life is hard, but God is good. Doing good is hard, but we aren't alone in the journey.

Perhaps you're reading this and your heart is pounding from the hardness of your good work, or your fear of the hardness paralyzes your good steps of faith. I have been there. I still quake, but I can say with certainty that we are never alone.

UNPINNED FAITH

Let me encourage you to dig deep into your heart. Galatians 6:9 has ministered to me: "Let us not become weary in doing good, for at the proper time we will reap a harvest if we do not give up." I love this verse because first it acknowledges that good work for God is exhausting. Can I get an amen? But if we keep going, if we refuse to throw in the towel, our good work will produce a harvest. As farmers who plant the seed and till the ground know, a bountiful crop isn't up to us. We do the work, God brings the results. All for His glory.

What are your fears today? Name them. They aren't nearly as scary when we put them at the feet of Jesus, who conquers all.

- How am I balancing my good work and my family?
- Am I taking time for my relationship with Jesus?
- I'm tired. How can I renew my strength? Try journaling or confide in a friend. Wait on Jesus and let Him renew you today.

CHAPTER 10

POWER OF ONE

✺

*I have learned that I will not change the world. Jesus will do that.
I can, however, change the world for one person. I can change the
world for fourteen little girls and for four hundred schoolchildren and
for a sick and dying grandmother and for a malnourished, neglected,
abused five-year-old. And if one person sees the love of Christ in me,
it is worth every minute. In fact, it is worth spending my life for.*

KATIE J. DAVIS

WHEN I SET OUT to do my one big thing for Jesus, I found out
just how small I really was. Charity, the second girl we brought
into Rehema House, came to us four months pregnant and
bitter. She didn't want to be in our home; she didn't want to
be rescued. She hated the unplanned pregnancy that was strip-
ping her of the education she desperately wanted. She hated
her unborn child. We rescued her to save the baby she wanted
to illegally abort.

Charity was an orphan, and the children's home that had taken
her in and was educating her swiftly kicked her out when they
discovered her pregnancy. She came to Mercy House because it
was better than being homeless. Her first months in our home
were hard. She was a survivor who had been on her own for
several years, and she bullied the other girls, picking fights and

mocking the staff. On more than one occasion we encouraged her to leave if she couldn't comply with the rules.

Sadly, she all but ignored her growing stomach, and when she gave birth to her son, Travis, the third baby born to our home, she despised him.

She didn't want to hold or look at him, breastfeed or mother her child. Our staff patiently urged her to love him. Weeks passed, and as Charity refused to take care of herself or her son, his health began to decline. She was an orphaned mother with a child's orphaned spirit.

I'll never forget Maureen's words over Skype one day: "The doctor has said the baby is not thriving due to the mother's lack of care. I am forcing her to feed the child and am filling in the gaps she leaves in his care. We need to fast and pray for a miracle."

And so we did, for days. I begged God for a bond, a covenant between mother and child. I was as desperate for Jesus to

Travis (18 months) and Charity

do a miracle as I was for my next breath. We didn't have a plan in place for a mom who didn't want her baby. We couldn't turn him over to a government orphanage. I knew deep down that this child was the answer to his orphaned mother's attachment issues. We read, prayed, cried, offered counseling. My goal has always been to be somewhat invisible to the residents in the maternity home, and instead of being seen as a hero, I want to empower Maureen and her staff. But in hard situations like these, I often feel so inadequate, an ocean apart and absolutely powerless. And I was. I hadn't morphed into an orphan specialist or supreme advocate; I was still a mom in Texas who said yes to something so much bigger than I was.

Maureen sent a few pictures of a group gathering a couple of weeks after our fast, and the first thing I noticed in the picture was the way Charity was looking at her son. Something had changed. I quickly e-mailed Maureen and asked her, and she responded, "Yes, God is doing something good in her heart."

ONE THING

I didn't step foot into my favorite store for six months after returning from my first trip to Kenya. I wasn't being a shopping martyr. I just couldn't remember why I'd spent so much time in a home decor store in the first place. If you could have seen my walls, you would have understood.

It was during the first year after starting Mercy House that I decided our family would wear only secondhand clothes and give only fair-trade gifts. I had become so aware of the plight of others that it spilled over into every area of my life. My kids carried backpacks made by refugees in Ecuador, my purse came from artisans in Uganda, and if my jewelry wasn't rolled paper, I didn't wear it. I spent a lot of time googling slave-free options. And then I learned about fair-trade chocolate. Was nothing safe?

I thought my new enlightenment was changing the world, but actually it was creating pressure and an unrealistic prison of self-sacrifice that made my family miserable. When Madison needed black dress pants for a band concert, instead of just finding the easiest option, I visited every resale shop in town and wasted a lot of time and energy. I ended up shopping where I should have in the first place.

One day a wise friend said to me (after hearing of my ridiculous time-consuming search for secondhand black pants), "What is your one thing?"

"What do you mean?" I asked cautiously.

"What is your passion? If you could pick one thing God has called you to do, what would it be? One."

I answered quickly because I had already defined it. "Encouraging mothers through my words and the work of Mercy House."

"Kristen, you're wasting a lot of time and energy trying to do it all. You're giving a lot, sacrificing your time building a home in Kenya. Don't let guilt rule you. Buy what you need and occasionally something you want, and if you can find them fair trade, awesome. But I think you might be all tangled up in good works."

I can't tell you how releasing her words were to me, opening that prison door. I thought about the hours I'd wasted searching for those silly black pants. I finally understood the old adage *Time is money* and vowed to spend that currency more carefully. I also realized I was in a danger zone. I was on the slippery slope of proving my goodness by doing good, which leads to self-righteousness. It was the kick in the pants I needed in order to remember who I was really working for.

Maybe your one thing is fair-trade clothes or teaching Sunday school. Perhaps it's the local homeless shelter, orphan care, adoption, or mentoring kids after school. I'm not saying we shouldn't be aware and generous in other areas. That's a given. I just think we shouldn't try to do it all because we are motivated by guilt.

Take adoption, for example. We are not all called to bring orphans into our homes, but caring for orphans (and widows) is a biblical mandate for believers (James 1:27). It's not optional. While we are doing that in Kenya, we are also buying cookies at a friend's fund-raiser to bring her child home from the Ukraine and donating garage sale items for another family's adoption sale. Your one thing might not be adoption, but that doesn't mean you shouldn't give to the couple in your church raising money to bring a baby home, host a fund-raiser, or become certified to offer respite care for foster families.

Because here's the real gift in that: finding and pursuing your one passion changes your life and ignites a godly desire to support others in their divine pursuits. When you get involved in someone else's God-sized dream, you are a part of his or her story.

I believe we are all called to do something, just not *everything*. Focusing on our one thing and doing it well to His glory is both liberating and life changing.

SMALL IS BIG

Picture a young girl living in a third-world country. She was from a simple home and an ordinary family, one that didn't put too much emphasis on material possessions. But as a part of their everyday life, they did what they could to care for the poor and oppressed. When this little girl was around eight years old, she told her dad she wanted to spend her life serving God and helping the poor. "If the thought of it makes you happy," her father responded, "you should do it. The deep inner joy that you feel is the compass that indicates the direction of your life."[1]

This little girl grew up to win countless awards for her prestigious work with the poor. Mother Teresa was one of the world's greatest women. She once said, "It is not how much we do, but how much love we put in the doing. It is not how much we give, but how much love we put in the giving."[2] She was a renowned world changer who was supported and propelled into her life of service by a strong family.

But there is only one Mother Teresa. There will never be another. And more than likely, we will never know the same fame (that she shunned) or have as far-reaching an impact.

World changers don't set out to the change the world; they see one need and do what they can to meet it. They usually don't even know they are changing the world. You might be thinking right now, *I will never be a world changer.* But I want to encourage you to change the way you see the power of one action done for someone else. When it's combined with the power of one big God, your small yes can change the world.

When I talk about my God-sized dream of working in Kenya, that's what God has called my family to do. It won't look the same for you, but your dream isn't any less significant or important. I received an e-mail one day from a sweet lady who wanted me to help her find a Leadership Development student like Maureen so she could start a maternity home too, in another third-world country. I encouraged her to let God show her the way and gently urged her not to re-create what looked successful. That is something that Mother Teresa stressed.

Stay where you are. Find your own Calcutta. Find the sick, the suffering, and the lonely right there where you are—in your own homes and in your own families, in your workplaces and in your schools. You can find Calcutta all over the world, if you have the eyes to see. Everywhere, wherever you go, you find people who are unwanted, unloved, uncared for, just rejected by society—completely forgotten, completely left alone.[3]

World changers all have one thing in common: they understand the power of one.

The mass of people, the enormous need around us is overwhelming. It's common to have the desire to do something but end up doing nothing because we don't know where to start. So we start with one: one tired teacher, one latchkey kid, one refugee, one person who needs a costly surgery. One.

Beth Clark, who helped Katie Davis tell her story in *Kisses from Katie*, has seen the power of one firsthand in Uganda.

People who really want to make a difference in the world usually do it, in one way or another. And I've noticed something about people who make a difference in the world: They hold the unshakable conviction that individuals are extremely important, that every life matters. They get excited over one smile. They are willing to feed one stomach, educate one mind, and treat one wound. They aren't determined to revolutionize the world all at once; they're satisfied with small changes. Over time, though, the small changes add up. Sometimes they even transform cities and nations, and yes, the world.[4]

It's vital we understand that every person was created for a specific purpose. And every family is made up of a group of unique people. There is only one family like yours. Think of the prostitute Rahab in the Bible: she is mentioned because she met a need. She wouldn't have considered herself a significant hero of the faith, and yet she changed the course of history because she let God use her insignificance to fulfill a specific purpose, a choice that placed her in the lineage of Jesus. Rahab is listed with Moses, David, Samson, and Samuel, all people with faith demonstrated by good deeds (Hebrews 11:31; James 2:25).

Perhaps you care for an elderly parent, hand-feeding him or her, serving in a quiet manner. Maybe your family encourages the new neighbor who is overwhelmed and alone, or maybe you volunteer at a local nonprofit, shipping packages. Glorious? No. Needed? Definitely.

We often don't do anything because we think our contribution won't be enough. Or we convince ourselves that we must do something great for it to be important. We don't act because we lack the confidence. We convince ourselves that our contribution couldn't possibly matter. This is a lie to keep us idle and focused on ourselves.

With the evolution of the Internet and social media, it's easy to get bogged down in an overwhelming number of cause-related opportunities. There are more than six billion people in the world today, each created with a purpose and a responsibility to fill a need. It might not be noteworthy or receive global recognition, but it matters. When it comes to building God's Kingdom, the "bigger is better" mentality doesn't apply. On the contrary, God often makes His glory known in the small and obscure. Look at the loaves-and-fishes story in John 6:10-13:

Jesus said, "Have the people sit down." There was plenty of grass in that place, and they sat down (about five thousand men were there). Jesus then took the loaves, gave thanks, and distributed to those who were seated as much as they wanted. He did the same with the fish.

When they had all had enough to eat, he said to his disciples, "Gather the pieces that are left over. Let nothing be wasted." So they gathered them and filled twelve baskets with the pieces of the five barley loaves left over by those who had eaten.

Most everyone has heard the story of how Jesus multiplied one boy's lunch of a few loaves and a couple of fish into something big enough to feed a massive crowd. I believe God is calling us, like the boy, to smallness—to give what we have in thankfulness and let Him to do the miraculous multiplication. Could manna have just fallen from the sky to feed the thousands? Of course. God has ultimate power. But He often chooses to work through us. He wants us to participate in the miracle.

I wonder about that little boy. Can you imagine how he felt? I know I would have been hesitant to offer my small gift to Jesus because I often buy into that size mentality of our culture. But look what God can do with one small gift.

One piece of fruit caused the fall of man. One righteous man built an ark. One stutterer delivered God's people from slavery. One shepherd boy brought down a giant and his army with one stone. One mother said yes to a miraculous pregnancy; one baby was born to rescue the world.

We aren't called to do big things; we are just called to do something that fulfills this command: Love God. Love others.

If you visited our home in Kenya today, you would discover there isn't a better mother than Charity. She takes pride in her son as he now toddles on the dusty path out to the playground. He is fat, healthy, and happy, and she adores him. He is a miracle. They are miraculous together, and their bond is strong.

Eighteen-year-old Charity's heart has been transformed. She says, "My relationship with my baby is fantastic since we get along very well. I really feel good when I see how my baby responds to corrections, and it makes me feel that I am a good mother." And she is in the process of building a future for them. She is taking full advantage of the high school we now offer in our home; she wants to be a newscaster someday.

Charity is only one girl in Kenya. Making a difference in her life may seem insignificant to others who look at the countless needs in this vast country riddled with extreme poverty and suffering. For every desperate pregnant girl we rescue, there are hundreds of others with similar needs. What we do feels small, too small most days. But Charity is going to change her country, one action at a time.

I have learned that small is big in God's economy. He tells us to look for the one lost lamb, even when there are ninety-nine others safe and sound in the fold.

❋ ❋ ❋

UNPINNED FAITH

Start small. Lay the burden of size aside and do the next small thing. It may seem insignificant, and perhaps it is, but what if it's the yes that leads to ten more? We all have a unique situation, and we can meet only the needs we know about. Pray and ask God for an opportunity to start somewhere.

Give what you have. Share it, even if what's in your hand is ridiculously tiny. Give it away. Ask God to multiply your gift . . . whether it be a talent, a desire, an open door, an opportunity, or a dollar. The gift isn't in what you give; it is in giving what you have.

Give the rest away. I wouldn't be writing this book or living this crazy life if I hadn't asked others to join me. I offered God what I had, which was very little, and then I shared the need with those around me so they could offer what they had too. Don't hold so tightly to your small thing or it will remain small. Open your hand and let others be a part of it.

Be faithful. No matter what happens, in greatness or smallness, don't give up. Be faithful in your task of following Jesus. You will never regret it.

Ask yourself:

- Am I pursuing my passion?
- What is my one thing?
- How can I engage in my community to help those around me pursue their one thing?

CHAPTER 11

JUST ANOTHER RICH MOM

✴

*It's not just the rich who get to give—it's all those who give who get to
be rich. You don't wait until you have more before you give to God—
you give now so you get to become more in God. . . . It's not having
much that makes you rich—it's the giving much that makes you rich.
Give and you are the rich.*

ANN VOSKAMP

WHEN I RETURNED to my comfortable American life, I discovered just how weighed down I was with stuff. Our two-
thousand-square-foot living space was crammed with enough
home accessories to cover several houses. My shopping had
become more than a hobby; somewhere it had turned into a
habit. I accumulated stuff—stuff that not only filled my home,
it cluttered *my heart.*

It wasn't just shopping and decorating that led to this over-
stuffed life, it was consumption. I was buying stuff out of bore-
dom. I would meander around Target, canvassing the clearance
aisles, and buy things I didn't need just because they were on
sale.

I pulled big plastic tubs from the attic and discovered I
could have decorated the entire street for Christmas. I asked

my neighbor if her two newly married daughters would like to freely shop from my excess. I piled up the wall hangings and rugs and dishes and more in the garage, and my family had a big garage sale. We donated the money to a charity, and it was liberating.

Stuff doesn't fill emptiness; it just hides it. When I looked at my life filled with wealth, I only saw poverty in my heart.

It was a terrible discovery.

For the first time, I understood the rich young ruler's choice in Mark 10:21-22.

> Jesus . . . said, "There's one thing left: Go sell whatever you own and give it to the poor. All your wealth will then be heavenly wealth. And come follow me."
>
> The man's face clouded over. This was the last thing he expected to hear, and he walked off with a heavy heart. He was holding on tight to a lot of things, and not about to let go. (*The Message*)

Sometimes the only way to change something that is wrong is to compare it to something right.

I was waking up from the American Dream that claimed I should have bigger and better and more for myself. I had tried that and only felt empty when I stood face-to-face with people who physically had nothing. Standing in the middle of extreme poverty, I discovered the kind of wealth I craved, and it had nothing to do with money.

When I arrived in Kenya in the spring of 2013 for a quick trip to meet a few new residents and oversee video production of a mini documentary, I was tired—the kind of exhaustion that comes from middle-of-the-night flights, crossing multiple time zones, and sleeping sitting up. Just hours after I landed in Nairobi, I sat in a Kenyan church service surrounded by the residents of Mercy House, worshiping the God who had rescued them from despair. I pinched myself awake because I didn't want to miss a moment of it.

At Rehema House a couple of the girls greeted me as family. "Mom Kristen, you are looking smart and very fat." Ah, there's nothing like a Kenyan compliment.

From previous visits, I knew that *smart* referred to "fashionable." I'll take that any day, and especially this one, considering I was wearing rubber boots and had dirty hair. I also knew that being called "fat," however hard it was to hear, meant you looked really healthy. The girls often referred to Terrell as fat, and I always giggled when I heard it. This was the first time I had been deemed "healthy looking" by them. That has not been true for most of them.

I have watched dangerously malnourished pregnant girls come into the maternity home and stare at their huge plates of food in disbelief. They were far from healthy or *fat*. Every pound they gained was a victory against their life of poverty and abiding hunger and a benefit to their unborn children. The staple starch of Kenya, along with many other African countries, is called *ugali*. It's made from maize (field corn) that is pounded to the consistency of flour and cooked to a thick mush. The mush makes you feel full, but it offers little nutritional value when you are malnourished.

In some ways, *ugali* might be considered an emotional "comfort food" to Africans because it's equated with a full stomach, something many people don't experience often. For many, it is the only food they eat. While we still serve *ugali* at the maternity home a couple of times a week because it's a favorite, it's not the main course. The residents feast on chicken, beef, fish, liver, fresh vegetables, lentils, and fruit.

"Look, Mom Kristen," said Sarah, one of the girls, as she patted her own tummy, "I'm getting fat too." The pride in her voice was unmistakable.

In that moment, I was ashamed. Did these girls understand that I came from a land of fat people? I'm referring not only to weight. I'm talking about how much we have in material possessions and yet live each day bloated by emptiness. We don't even realize it until we see people with so little. I am not saying that we don't have poverty in the United States. But even people who lack financial means have something that developing and third-world countries don't have: opportunity. It's vastly different in countries where welfare and government aid don't exist. Many people in the world don't have consistent access to basic needs like clean water and food.

It dawned on me that having enough to eat every day and being able to provide enough food for my family not only made me healthy—it made me rich. Most of us in the States don't think of ourselves as wealthy, but if you can afford to buy this book instead of food, you're in the top percentage of wealthy people in the world.

HOW RICH AM I?

If you're juggling car payments and a mortgage and trying to squeeze more money out of your month, you might be thinking, *I am not rich!* I know I would have laughed if you'd told me that when our family of four was living on a one-income youth pastor's salary. In reality, instead of comparing ourselves to our neighbors and friends, we should compare ourselves to the world.

According to GivingWhatWeCan.org, you can discover just how rich you are. Let's say your family of four lives on $30,000 a year total income. That's not exactly wealthy by American standards, right? Well, with that amount of income, you are in the richest 14 percent of the world's population. Double it to $60,000 a year and you're in the top 6 percent of richest families in the world.[1]

HOW POOR IS THE WORLD?

It's shocking when you read global poverty facts and discover how the rest of the world really lives:

- Did you know that 80 percent of the world's population lives on less than $10.00 per day?
- Half the world lives on less than $2.50 a day.
- The poorest 40 percent of the world's population accounts for 5 percent of global income. The richest 20 percent accounts for three-quarters of world income.
- Twenty-two thousand children die every day due to poverty-related reasons.
- Around 27 to 28 percent of all children in developing countries are estimated to be underweight or stunted.[2]

I'm not an expert on the economy, global issues, or even cooking, for that matter. But I do believe that if we understand how much we have and how much others lack, not only will it make us more grateful, it will make the needs around us more visible. Giving What We Can, the international society dedicated to eliminating poverty in the developing world, has raised that kind of awareness. "Our wealth is largely due to the fact that we have been born in wealthy countries benefiting from good institutions. This inequality, however, gives us the capacity to achieve a lot for others: by giving a small fraction of our income, we can raise the income of the world's poorest disproportionately. By concentrating on the most cost-effective charities, we can achieve even more."[3]

Here's what I've learned since being involved in Mercy House: it's not really about who is poor and who is rich because poverty and wealth aren't really about money or things. It comes down to contentment. I've taken people with me to Kenya who want to buy a washing machine for the maternity home and a "real broom" to use for sweeping because they don't understand the culture. The home doesn't need an electric washing machine. Our residents need to know how to do laundry by hand because that's how laundry is done in their homes. And when they bend over to sweep with a collection of sticks, they don't need a different broom. We can't fix what's not broken. Most of the things we think would improve their lives are actually conveniences; things like microwaves and Crock-Pots and air-conditioning can make life easier, but not necessarily better.

Steve Saint, who lived with the Waodani tribe in the jungles of Ecuador, understands this:

Among people living simply amidst abundant resources, poverty is not measured in annual income or net worth, but in "what I have in comparison to what those around me have." In such contexts poverty is more of an attitude and a mood than an actual state of having or not having something. In such contexts, contentment is the secret. Some people think 1 Timothy 6:6 says "Godliness is a means of gain," but really it says, "Godliness with contentment is great gain." Where there is godliness with contentment there is no perceived "poverty" until discontentment has been stirred.[4]

✳

Maureen visited my family in America for the first time in 2013.

We pulled into the driveway, and I put my van in park and hit my garage door opener. As we unbuckled our seat belts, Maureen looked into my garage and then looked at me. "Mom, I didn't know your family also sold bicycles." She was pointing at the five bikes hanging from hooks in our garage. Her words shook me to the core.

I was so embarrassed. She looked into my messy, disorganized garage, cluttered with a lawn mower, basketballs, and shelves full of tools and supplies, and saw wealth. I saw the garage as a big honey-do list.

Maureen hadn't even been inside my home, and I was already convicted.

For the next few weeks, I saw my life the way she saw it and realized just how much I had, and even more, how much I take for granted on a daily basis. From cooking to cleaning, my home is filled with modern conveniences I've always had—hot water on tap that doesn't have to be boiled before I use it, canned food, a stove that doesn't require charcoal or a tank of propane at my feet—the list is endless. Maureen would watch me closely, and we would talk about the contrasts between her home and mine. Maureen marveled that I could prepare a healthy meal in thirty minutes. With her standing in my kitchen, it was easy to swallow my normal complaints about what to cook for dinner or that I had to cook at all. We openly talked about the differences, and Maureen never condemned our way of life as she tried to understand it. At the same time, I like the conveniences in our culture, and Maureen could understand why.

Maureen at Chick-fil-A

It was fun to expose her to new things in our country. For lunch one day, I took her to Chick-fil-A around the corner from our house. She had tasted "Christian Chicken" as she calls it during her stay with Student Life and loves it as much as I do. I always tuck chicken sauces into a suitcase when I visit so she can have a "taste of home." As we were eating, the Chick-fil-A mascot showed up. Maureen's reaction was hilarious—she was so confused. When the Chick-fil-A "cow" hugged Maureen in the restaurant, she was shaking from fright because she didn't believe it wasn't real. During her visit, she fell in love with Chinese food and decided we should eat it every day. I took her roller skating for the first time with my kids, and we laughed so hard at her trying to get the hang of it. I took her to Target and bought her some new clothes and shoes, and she fit perfectly into our family.

As we drove through my town, she kept remarking on all

the pet stores, vets, and animal clinics. I didn't dare take her into PetSmart or tell her that the people in my country spent more than $53 billion on their pets in 2011.[5] She wanted to know where all the hospitals and clinics for people were located. In her country, there are medical facilities on nearly every street, with most patients sharing beds because sick people outnumber open beds. I tried to explain about medical insurance and preventative healthcare, but the more I talked, the more hollow my answers sounded.

At one point she said, "Do your people not know how my people live?"

I quietly answered, "Many don't want to know." And I couldn't help but think of my own choice to be ignorant for most of my adult life.

Often what we need is a perspective change. It's so easy to get caught up in consumerism and ungratefulness. Someone once said, "People who look through keyholes are apt to get the idea that most things are keyhole shaped."

A few years ago, I was outside pulling weeds, and when my neighbor saw me, she invited me in to see her beautiful remodeled house that was finally complete. Now, these were friends who loved God, served on staff at a church, and had lived in their home more than twenty years. They had finally paid the last payment and owned their house. They deserved a little update, in my opinion.

When I walked through their door and saw their gorgeous wood floors, I fell in love. I finished the tour and complimented her on the beautiful renovation, then headed back home. As soon as I opened the door, this came out of my mouth: "We need wood floors too."

I didn't even know I wanted them until I saw my neighbor's.

I immediately compared my lack to her gain. Isn't that human nature? (I never did get those wood floors, but just between you and me, I still would like to have them.) Perhaps you've done the same with a girlfriend's new dress or a friend's new car. When I stood in a mud hut in the middle of extreme poverty, I found myself making comparisons too, but with the opposite effect. It all depends on how you look at it.

In Matthew 26:11, Jesus says that the poor will always be with us. I don't think we can cure world poverty by changing our perspective or through charitable giving. Pastor Kevin DeYoung writes,

> The Christian needs to be generous, but generous charity is not the answer to the world's most pressing problems of hunger, inadequate medical care, and grinding poverty. Wealth is created in places where the rule of law is upheld, property rights are secured, people are free to be entrepreneurs, and there is sufficient social capital to encourage risk-taking. We can and should do good with our giving. But we must not lead people to believe that most of human suffering would be alleviated if we simply gave more.[6]

It's not about giving all our money away and living with the poor like Mother Teresa (unless God specifically calls us to do so). It's about (1) being willing to do just that if He asks, and (2) exchanging our poverty of spirit that is often found in consumerism for abundant joy, which is often discovered in relentless generosity.

On a daily basis I race from Internet meetings with coworkers in Kenya to the school carpool line in America. One minute I'm trying to help a fourteen-year-old girl escape from sex trafficking and the next, I'm listening to my own fourteen-year-old daughter tell me all her friends have iPhones and hair highlights. One of my greatest challenges is living with one foot in the first world and the other in the third. And while I can't ultimately change either or all, I can live with intention, and that's what changes me, my family, and maybe the world. Elizabeth Dreyer, in her book *Earth Crammed with Heaven*, makes this provocative statement: "In a profound way, our intentionality is a key ingredient determining whether we notice God everywhere or only in church or only in suffering, or nowhere. It all depends on how we choose to fashion our world."[7] When we open our eyes to what we have and how others live, it affects the choices we make.

WE CAN BE CONSCIENTIOUS CONSUMERS

Before my youngest started her last year of preschool, we went shoe shopping. She walked right over to the row of sparkly tennis shoes and declared, "I want Twinkle Toes." At the time, I hadn't heard much about these light-up, overpriced shoes, but she begged and pleaded, and I gave in. She did need shoes, and they were 20 percent off (and she was my baby and, honestly, I didn't want a tantrum in the middle of the mall. I never said I was perfect).

A few weeks later, she excitedly told me she was a part of a club on the playground. "Mommy, it's called the Twinkle Toe Club. Only girls with sparkly shoes are allowed in it."

Oh my word. Later I saw commercials for these silly shoes on TV in between kids' shows. My daughter danced and twirled to the advertisement. I turned off the TV and realized I had been suckered into consuming something based on a buck—apparently so had a lot of other moms—and tried to introduce my preschooler to the concept of buying what we need instead of what everyone else has.

Media not only targets our children and homes, it influences what we buy. Jim Taylor, the author of *Raising Generation Tech*, sounded the alarm in an article in the *Huffington Post*.

> Popular culture is big business, to the tune of $1.2 billion a year. . . . Research has also shown that in the United States, children have influence over their family's food and drink purchases, purchases totaling 100 billion dollars each year. Popular culture wants you to raise consumers, not children! . . . Popular culture is now so ubiquitous, intense and unrelenting that if your children are exposed to it without sufficient limits or guidance, it will go far beyond simple entertainment and become a powerful—and unhealthy—influence on them.[8]

When we consider where the shoes and clothes and cheap jewelry we love to wear come from, it's quite revealing. And disturbing. As I write these words, news programs are talking about the horrific sewing factory collapse in Bangladesh that killed more than a thousand people. No doubt something in my closet came from this oppressed country. Cheap clothes come at a high price.

So what do we do?

I've been down the confusing and hard-to-follow road of trying to buy only fair-trade or secondhand clothes, among other things. I am not advocating boycotting clothes made in other countries. I am encouraging conscientious shopping. Here are some ideas to get you started:

- *Turn off the TV.* Your family is being targeted through advertisements. The best way to fight it is by tuning it out. Mute or fast-forward through commercials and be aware of TV's influence in your home.
- *Ask questions.* We sell fair-trade items our residents make in the Mercy Shop (shop.mercyhousekenya.org), an online store that benefits each of our girls' futures. In the early days, I carried stylish shirts and cute bags imprinted with our website address as a fund-raiser. One day it dawned on me that I had no idea who was actually making these items. I lost a lot of sleep wondering if in an effort to set girls free we were keeping others in bondage. I was finally able to verify that the items were made in factories that were compliant with fair-trade standards, but I learned a valuable lesson: ask first.
- *Look for alternatives.* We were able to find a fair-trade company (FreesetGlobal.com) to purchase some of our bags and shirts to resell as a fund-raiser. The shirts cost a bit more, but each purchase provides a job for women rescued from sex trafficking. Now when people support Mercy House, they are also supporting women in India.
- *Educate yourself and your children.* Watch documentaries, read news reports, and Google stores for information. My teen daughter loves fashion and accessories. She also loves the residents of Mercy House and understands human trafficking and cheap labor. We've talked enough about slavery in our world today for her to understand

a "deal" isn't always as good as it seems, and I, in turn, am raising a future shopper who will hopefully influence her peers to do the same. To learn more, check out the information gathered by the US Department of Labor that lists goods produced by child or forced labor at www.dol.gov/ilab/programs/ocft/PDF/2011TVPRA.pdf.

- *Beware of cheap finds.* I love a good sale! While I'm not saying everything inexpensive is produced by slave labor or that it's wrong to purchase, proceed with caution on the cheap deals. I can't trace everything I wear to where it is made. I simply don't have the time. (That's not my one thing, remember?) But if it's too cheap to believe, it has probably cost someone something. When in doubt, buy homemade, handcrafted, or cause-related.

WE CAN LIVE GENEROUSLY

Generous people raised me. My parents are two of the most giving people I know. From early childhood to today, they have freely given what they have to others in need. They have repaired cars, paid bills, helped missionaries, funded projects, bought appliances—the list is endless. It's also inspiring and contagious. I can remember from a young age hearing my dad say, "You can't outgive God," and I watched as he opened one hand to give to others and opened the other to receive from God. My dad once emptied our family savings account to give it away, and we watched God replace every dime. This picture of open hands for giving and receiving shaped me. We can all be part of that conduit, standing in the middle between God and people in need, ready to give spontaneously.

I want this for my children. I want them to see us give a family in need a generous check, offer to help a friend, see the joy in giving big to the teachers in our lives. I want to look for opportunities to involve my children in generosity. I tell them stories of other kids who are giving, not to make them feel guilty, but to inspire them to action.

Not long ago, our six-year-old did just that. After hearing a story about a generous child, she said, "I want to do that." We sat down as a family and talked about a few needs we were aware of, and our children chose to help start a small business for friends in Kenya. We discussed various ways to raise the money, and a garage sale won out. Our kids each contributed items from their rooms, and my little girl sorted and helped separate donations from our community group and learned the fine art of garage sale pricing. Our kids "helped" run the sale— if you have kids, you know that means they played with all the toys they donated and even bought a few back. Baby steps. The money raised bought two sewing machines to start a business in another country.

By far, one of the greatest and most powerful lessons I've been taught in this journey is the beauty and life change that comes from being generous.

I hold fast to Winston Churchill's words: "We make a living by what we get; we make a life by what we give."[9]

Christmas is a golden opportunity to help others. A few years ago, I wanted my kids to fall in love with the joy of giving. Terrell and I took them to Target and told them to pick out an age-appropriate toy to give to the kids of a single mom in our church. At first it was hard for them, standing there in the toy aisle, looking longingly at the colorful, fun items that would have been nice on their own wish lists. But then they really got into it and ended up putting way more items in the basket than we had planned.

A week before Christmas, we each wrapped a gift or two, then drove across town to deliver the packages. We saw that the mom had left her garage open, and while the rest of us hid in the car in the dark, Terrell snuck the big box of gifts into the open garage and quietly placed them next to her van. We giggled and hushed our voices, although the excitement was tangible. We circled the block three times to see if our anonymous gifts had been discovered yet, but they were untouched. We left, hoping she would discover them (and her open garage door) before morning.

Back home, as the kids got ready for bed, we all speculated on how shocked the family would be. I happened to check Facebook (I'm friends with this lady and am probably totally "outing" myself all these years later), and when I read her status update, I rushed upstairs to share with the kids her excitement, joy, tears, and relief for this unexpected surprise.

I will never forget the look of pride on their faces. They never told a soul about what we did on that December night, but they have never forgotten how good it felt to give.

❋

A couple of years ago, my pastor issued a challenge to our congregation: "Look at your life and where you have in abundance, even excess. Is it toys bursting from the playroom, clothes in the closet, food in the pantry, an extra car in the garage? Take seven days and ask God to reveal someone who is lacking in the area of your abundance. And then share what you have."

It's what Jesus talks about in Matthew 25:35-40.

> "I was hungry and you fed me,
>   I was thirsty and you gave me a drink,
>   I was homeless and you gave me a room,
>   I was shivering and you gave me clothes,
>   I was sick and you stopped to visit,
>   I was in prison and you came to me."
>
> Then those "sheep" are going to say, "Master, what are
> you talking about? When did we ever see you hungry and
> feed you, thirsty and give you a drink? And when did we
> ever see you sick or in prison and come to you?" Then the
> King will say, "I'm telling the solemn truth: Whenever
> you did one of these things to someone overlooked or
> ignored, that was me—you did it to me." (*The Message*)

We don't give because we have a lot. We give because we've
been given a lot to give away.

A generous person is always ready to spontaneously give to
those in need. It's usually inconvenient and unplanned. It will
probably cost us comfort, even pride. It won't be easy or bring
us fame.

This is Christianity.

UNPINNED FAITH

When our worldview is altered by realizing how much we have
in comparison with how little others have, it opens up a whole

new world of opportunity for us. We have been given much, and much is required of us. Here are some practical questions to ask yourself:

- What shopping choices can you make to become a more conscientious consumer?
- How rich are you? Take the challenge: look at the excess in your life and ask God to help you find someone to share it with.
- How can you live more generously?

CHAPTER 12

DEFEATING MY BIGGEST FOES

✳

When gratitude to God revolutionizes your life, God uses you to
revolutionize the world. It's why God said to give thanks in everything.

ANN VOSKAMP

THE MOMENT I SAW IT, I fell in love with it. I had always wanted a red couch, and we had saved and saved for it. It was the first piece of furniture we bought for our first house in Texas. The couch's floral pillows looked perfect against the red pinstripes. From the moment it was delivered, we began a comfy history together. I read countless books to my kids sitting on that sofa and had meaningful conversations curled up on it with Terrell. Even after our evil dog, Katie, chewed the skirt off the front and we loaded it in our van and had an upholstery shop remove the fabric skirt off the back and reattach it to the front and shoved it against the living room wall, I still loved it. It was my favorite piece of furniture until our cat, Ike, peed all over it, and then it was dead to me.

If they didn't behave, the pets would be next. And I'll just confess right now that at this point in our lives, we had begun to number our pets instead of name them.

We cleaned the couch and made do for a while by turning the cushions over, but cat pee is like spoiled milk—the odor never really goes away. Every time I thought about getting another couch, I second-guessed myself. We were in the middle of starting Mercy House and were being extra careful with money in case our God-sized dream backfired. Every time we talked about buying a new one, we thought about the sofa we had sat on during a home visit in Kenya. It was tattered and old and bricks held up one leg.

I felt guilty.

I don't know about you, but guilt is something I struggled with even before I became a mother. I think it started in the bathroom of a seafood restaurant when I had morning sickness at lunch. Between waves of nausea, I read the warning signs not to eat seafood while pregnant. Oops.

Guilty—even without being charged.

Mom guilt is common and often a daily companion. We are multitasking doers, and we have high expectations for ourselves. When our reality (sick kids and muddy dogs) overrides our expectations, we're disappointed in who we are and what we've accomplished.

When my first baby was born, I took scrapbooking classes. I spent countless hours cutting out tiny shapes and letters from colored card stock, spelling out precious baby words. The carefully crafted book covers the first five years of Madison's life. Jon-Avery's scrapbook is not quite as detailed, has store-bought stickers, and ends on his third birthday. And then there's the baby of the family, who isn't much of a baby any more.

Emerson's seven years old, and her book documents the first six months of her life haphazardly, with stacks of pictures and mementos in ziplock plastic bags somewhere in the attic.

Out of the blue the other day, I had a panicky moment thinking about how little I'd done on my youngest's book. Before I knew it, instead of making dinner, I was digging out old (as in five years) scrapbook paper and stickers and spreading them all over my bed. My kids walked in after school and asked what I was doing. I have had their books hidden away for years, but one thing led to another, and before I knew it, we were all sitting around laughing and pointing at cute baby bottoms. And then the inevitable happened: my youngest wanted to know why there wasn't much to look at in her baby book. And where were her cute locks of baby hair from her first haircut? Busted.

My fourteen-year-old helped me put several pages together quickly while I made up a lot of facts to fill in the blanks. Seriously, I'm over forty and I can't remember to take my Vitamin B shot, much less how much my child weighed at nine months old. So I had to lie. And then before I could stop myself, I snipped a small piece of my daughter's hair while I was pretending to fix it and put it in an envelope marked First Haircut.

I know. I am a horrible mother. See what I mean about The Guilt?

When I found this quote, it lightened my heavy load: "Memo to Moms: Relax! Research shows that not every little thing you do impacts how your kids will turn out—just being there for them makes the biggest impact of all."[1] (Thank you, Sharon Begley!)

Remember my epiphany moment on the playground when

another mom told me what kids really want from their moms? The answer was you. Their mom. Your kids just want you. It's true. Take a deep breath with me and give yourself a break. Guilt is not from God. He guides and corrects us, but He isn't the author of condemnation. When it's all said and done, with our successes and failures, our families just need us to be there for them.

That being said, when we start comparing ourselves to those with less, guilt is often on the heels of awareness. It's hard not to feel guilty about every purchase we make in the face of hungry children in our world or desperate pregnant girls.

One day after a heart-to-heart with Terrell (not on the couch but about it), we concluded we were giving and doing what God asked us to, and we decided if we could buy a new couch and continue our level of giving, we would. And we did. Since then, we've made other big purchases, but we try to have the need-versus-want conversation. Honestly, it's still a struggle. But I think it's supposed to be.

When I ran into an old friend in the spaghetti aisle at the grocery store, she hugged me and said, "How was your trip to Kenya? Was it just ah-*maazing*?!" She pulled the last syllable like taffy and her voice went up—I could almost see the exclamation points from her tone.

Before I could answer, she continued, her arms sweeping over the wide selection of food around us, "I bet you just want to give all this up and move there!"

I was momentarily speechless. Then I opened my mouth. What I meant to say was, "Yes, we had some amazing moments. But it was also *hard*." What came out was, "On my last day in Kenya, I convinced one of our girls not to run away with her tiny baby, lost track of when my family had showered last, and counted the hours until we boarded the plane. Oh, and we saw a dead man who had been run over in the middle of the road."

She couldn't grab her pasta fast enough.

I am not good at any of this. When I'm home surrounded by comfort, I long to be there. I get sick of all the stuff and pressure and complications of living first world. When I'm in Kenya—tangled in a mosquito net, covered in dust, wondering if we will have water for showers, and out of my comfort zone in a hundred ways—I revel in the simplicity of life and how close God is, but I long for America.

I try to wipe away the stain of the human suffering I have witnessed. I try to forget the world that didn't even pause when a man died after a hit-and-run in front of our van on the way to the airport. But I can't. It's as much a part of me now as my memories from our family vacation to Disney World.

In other words, I struggle.

Some days I feel angry, mad at how our world just continues in abundance, spending money on meaningless things as if there isn't epic human suffering happening simultaneously. I am ashamed at the relief I feel when I am home, how much I love the ease, comfort, and convenience in America. I am mad that I long for both worlds. I hunger for this while I ache for that.

Sometimes I think I initially said yes to my God-sized dream because of guilt and my fix-it way of thinking. I am slow to take credit for what has been accomplished in the last few years because it was all God and just a speck of me.

It all comes down to this question: *Do I love my comfort more than Christ?*

I get a different answer every day. But I believe we need to struggle. Because if we aren't struggling against our culture, we are giving in to it. Struggle brings gratitude. It makes us aware of things we often take for granted.

I think the following definition of *struggle* hits the nail on the head.

Struggle is the food from which change is made, and the best time to make the most of a struggle is when it's right in front of your face. Now, I know that might sound a bit simplistic. But too often we're led to believe that struggling is a bad thing, or that we struggle because we're doing something wrong. I disagree. I look at struggle as an opportunity to grow. True struggle happens when you can sense what is not working for you and you're willing to take the appropriate action to correct the situation. Those who accomplish change are willing to engage the struggle.[2]

I know I'm not alone. Maybe you feel it too. A friend of mine struggled after she and her husband bought a home. "I don't like the way the house looks. It's got old, stretched out, stained carpet and white walls. . . . When we bought the house, I had fully planned on taking up the carpet and refinishing the wood floors underneath as well as putting a fresh coat of paint on all the walls, which is purely a vain desire. But nothing *needs* to be changed or updated . . . not even close. All day today, I have fasted from Pinterest or even thinking about home decor, and I honestly can't decide if I'm being sinful or not in wanting those things. So my question is this: if you were in the same position, would you refinish the floors and paint the walls, or would you invest the money in Mercy House?"

Yes.

"In my opinion, I don't think it's wrong to paint or update some," I said. "I think it's wrong to go into debt to do it or to ignore the nudge to give to someone because you want things for yourself. Be generous givers and do the work of God and also set aside money to do good things for your family."

If it were us, we would give money to Mercy House and we would paint and maybe pull up carpet at some point. The bottom line for us is this: we feel good about what we are giving and doing for God (and if we don't, something is wrong). We hold our money loosely. If God lays it on our hearts to give someone money, we do it. But at the same time we also get what we need and occasionally what we want. And we struggle. Does God ask us to lay aside our plans to get something we want in order to provide for someone in need? Absolutely. We need to heed that call. We never regret giving, but we also don't want to be slaves to guilt.

David Platt says we need to stop producing low-level guilt in ourselves by asking unhealthy questions such as "What do I need to do, how do I need to give, or where do I need to go in order to do enough for God?"

The gospel teaches us that Christ alone is able to do enough. He alone has been faithful enough, generous enough, compassionate enough, etc. The gospel beckons our sin-sick souls to simple trust in Christ, the only One who is truly radical enough. In him, we no longer live from a position of guilt, but from a position of righteousness. . . . The message of Christianity is not that we need to do more for God, but that we need to trust in what God has done for us.[3]

And so we keep on doing work for Jesus and we keep on struggling. But most days we do so without the heavy weight of guilt.

✳

Our family was driving home from church one Sunday when Madison asked from the backseat, "Mom, who are your best friends?"

"You mean besides your dad?" I asked. I immediately named my mom and sister.

She laughed and said, "Besides them, too. Name five friends you can tell anything to, people who know you really well."

After naming three others, I stopped. I would have added my sister-in-law Rhonda to the list, but she had died a few months earlier from complications related to diabetes. And then I started crying, right there in the car.

I assured my daughter it wasn't her question that was upsetting me. I think it just dawned on me that I had lost one of the few people who knew me well and loved me just the way I am.

I'm an introvert. I like being alone. I crave quiet. I love people, too—just not too many at once, please. I am drained in a crowd and energized when I'm by myself. I used to think this was why I always struggled with loneliness. Well, that and mean girls. I was the girl who hung out with guy friends. When my husband became my best friend, I isolated myself even more from women. It seemed an easy way to guard my heart.

Now that I'm raising daughters who are becoming young

women, I am learning even more about myself. Two weeks before Madison started junior high, we attended orientation. Not only was she going to a new school—it was a new school in a new town where she didn't know a soul. I was terrified for her!

At orientation we had seen a notice about a back-to-school band pool party. Madison was in band, so we thought it would be a great place to meet new friends before the first day of classes. She seemed excited about it, but I wasn't certain she was up for this—or perhaps it was my own fear I was sensing.

"Are you sure you want to go?" I asked my daughter again. "You don't have to."

She nodded confidently, but I heard a catch in her voice when she asked, "Will you go with me?"

We talked about what to expect as she nervously held cupcakes on her lap (flute players were supposed to bring a dessert). I watched her take a deep breath as she opened the door to the natatorium and stepped into the unknown. Her hope outweighed her fear.

She put the dessert on the food table and then set her swim bag down, pulled off her cover-up, and got in line for the diving board. She left me in the bleachers, watching and wringing my hands. A big group of laughing girls walked past her without a second glance. She dove in and I prayed. I looked around for other moms of possible new girls to try to strike up a conversation and find my daughter a friend that way, but everyone was in their own little groups.

My mind flashed back to when I was her age and I was the outsider at school, so lonely it physically hurt. I saw my daughter searching for me in the stands, so I quickly swiped away my tears and smiled at her. I hoped she could see on my face what I felt in my heart. *I'm proud of you for trying. Being the new girl is so hard, but I know this will get better. Don't let this make you feel like you aren't enough—cool enough, smart enough, pretty enough. You are enough, just the way you are, and other girls will recognize that eventually.* And I tried to believe my own words.

I didn't want her to see how hard it was for me to watch her live this moment. I still fight fear whenever I'm in situations where I'm the "new girl"; I have to talk myself into sticking with it instead of bolting. When Madison came over, shivering, I was tempted to suggest running away. Wrapping her in a towel, I saw disappointment instead of hope in her eyes. She bit her lip, refusing to cry.

"Do you want to go home?" I asked softly.

"No. Not yet." She headed back to the pool. She wasn't ready to give up, and when she stepped back in the water, I wanted to stand up and cheer for my courageous daughter. For another painful thirty minutes she did everything in her power to meet people as the angst-filled memories of my junior high, high school, college, first job, church women's groups, and blogging conferences nearly sent me into a panic attack.

Finally, the ordeal was over. Madison couldn't hide the letdown, but she kept thanking me for being there, for not leaving her alone. I confessed all of my "new girl" experiences to her and we laughed together. As we walked to the car, she held my hand and consoled me, "Now I know how new kids feel, Mom. I'm not sorry I went. I will make friends. It's going to be okay." Where did such wisdom come from?

"You're never alone," I said, trying to imprint it on her soul. But I went to bed crying and praying that her words would come true. And they did. She didn't let the experience at the pool party sway her resolve to keep trying. She became the top flutist in her school, made the basketball team, received numerous awards, and made the junior honor society, but most important, she made friends that year.

The truth is that I need to take lessons from my daughter. Chasing a God-sized dream has alienated me even more from people than when I was wearing my Jesus pin. I quickly discovered that advocating for the poor makes some people feel uncomfortable. I went through a hard season of loneliness after going public with our desire to start a maternity home in Kenya. It sounded crazy, and there were people who chose not to dream with us. And that's okay. I can't blame them really. But with my tendency to isolate myself, it made my loneliness even more tangible.

Community has wounded me. I bet it has you, too. Friends who don't stick around when you go through hard times, girl-friends who gossip about you instead of gather around you. Basically, if you're breathing, you've been hurt by another person.

But in the same way, God has used community to heal me. He circled our family with supportive and loving people to help accomplish something bigger than us.

So why do I feel alone some days? It's a weak spot for me. It's a gap in the armor where I am attacked by the enemy most often. The funny thing is, I've never been alone. From my wild-for-Jesus teenage days to today, not only has God been with me every step of the way, He has orchestrated my life to include amazing people. In every season, I can look back and see a constant friend or family member who walked with me in the valleys and mountaintops. Still, I know I have a tendency to let loneliness rule the day, so I shouldn't be surprised when it surfaces. But it does, time and again. Just last week, I felt slighted when I wasn't invited to something I am passionate about and feel qualified for.

Here's how I handle it: I have learned to let people in. I have a few friends who know me very well, enough to push past any barriers I may erect or to help me come up for air when I pull into myself. One of those friends is my husband. Last week, I shared with Terrell my disappointment about not being invited to be part of a discussion on maternal health care with a group of women; his listening ear was a big encouragement. But ultimately, I always come back to the same answer—Jesus loves me and I am enough just as I am. He is my constant and He is with me always.

❋

We started Mercy House with nothing. We didn't have money or experience or a plan. We didn't have a staff, a house, or any inkling of what to do next. We had a simple idea to help girls. It was just a tiny seed.

When I look at what has sprouted from our yes, I am dumbfounded. It's simply breathtaking to see our busy home in Kenya (that we own debt free despite that country's expensive housing market, with plans underway to purchase another), bustling with dozens of girls and babies. I can only stand back and say, "Look what God has done."

Just six months before we purchased the home in Kenya, it seemed absolutely impossible but incredibly necessary. After two years of renting a home in Nairobi, we were at the mercy of a landlord who continued to raise the rent while refusing to provide what he'd promised in maintenance. Buying a permanent home in a city that comprises both extreme poverty and extreme wealth left our little organizations needing a miracle. The asking price for the house we were renting was one million US dollars, and land was even more expensive. Maureen and I prayed that God would somehow multiply our $100,000 seed money we'd been saving for a future home, given by moms and families. We talked and looked at every angle and asked God for the impossible, but in my heart I just couldn't see a way. Maureen spent

some weeks gathering information about available houses and discovered a home priced at $250,000 with a determined seller. It was still out of our range, but we were getting closer. I fretted and worried and again, doubted.

Rehema House

Meanwhile, Maureen negotiated fiercely and got the asking price down to $188,000.

And then an unexpected donation of $50,000 cash was given.

And another for $38,000 a month later.

And just like that, the impossible was possible.

Every step of the way, from fund-raising on my blog, to speaking, to visiting the devastating poverty our residents' families still live in, God has been faithful. I can't take credit for the good things He has done. This helps when the struggles come—and they do—constantly and without restraint. When I don't know what to do, I remind myself whom all this belongs to.

But I still doubt.

I'm almost ashamed to admit it. When I look ahead at what we still need to accomplish, how what we've done is just a small drop in a vast ocean of suffering, I am overwhelmed. As we dig deeper to help more girls, the problems only become bigger. It's more than I can handle most days as I try to figure out the next step, encourage and support Maureen in Kenya, raise more money to help more girls . . . it's just endless.

When I look too far ahead, I am filled with doubt and worry, and I am faithless.

God is constantly reminding me to look behind, to look at how far He has brought us, how many miracles He's performed along the way, how many mountains He's moved on our behalf, how many times He's rescued and healed, how much hope He has given. Even if I don't want it, I have His full attention. I turn to the words of the psalmist and read,

> GOD, investigate my life;
>> get all the facts firsthand.
> I'm an open book to you;
>> even from a distance, you know what I'm thinking.
> You know when I leave and when I get back;
>> I'm never out of your sight.
> You know everything I'm going to say
>> before I start the first sentence.
> I look behind me and you're there,
>> then up ahead and you're there, too—
>> your reassuring presence, coming and going.
> This is too much, too wonderful—
>> I can't take it all in!
>
> PSALM 139:1-6, *The Message*

When I look behind me, I see Jesus. When I do what He has called me to today, He is here. When I look to the future, He is there.

I love how Matt Redman reminds us of that in his song "Never Once." The words of the chorus resonate and have comforted me countless times: "Never once did we ever walk alone / Never once did You leave us on our own / You are faithful, God."

We don't know what the future holds. It may be filled with heartache or it may contain joy. Odds are it will have both. No matter what Jesus has done in my life, I tend to be faithless, full of guilt, loneliness, and doubt. But I can bank on one thing: He is faithful.

UNPINNED FAITH

In the last few years, I've acquired a firsthand education in extreme poverty and the profound impact of seeing babies live who were supposed to die. But my enemy isn't a lack of funds, a web of government paperwork, or even inexperience; it's *me*. And it's the same enemy that has reared its ugly head since I was that awkward girl in school wearing a sparkly pin. From guilt to loneliness to doubt, my mind is where Satan attacks hardest.

In 2 Corinthians 12:9, the apostle Paul reminds us that God works best in our weakness, a promise He makes to all of His children. "'My grace is sufficient for you, for my power is made perfect in weakness.' Therefore I will boast all the more gladly of my weaknesses, so that the power of Christ may rest upon me" (ESV).

What voices are trying to discourage you today? Remember,

- It's okay to admit our weaknesses. It's more dangerous to keep them hidden. Naming them is a step to quieting them.
- Oftentimes our biggest enemy is the feeling of inadequacy. Do you feel like you aren't good enough or that your life is simply too messy to do anything for God? God isn't waiting for us to have a perfect life; He's waiting on us to say yes.
- Your weakness is the perfect place for God's glory. Instead of seeing your weakness as an "I can't," see it as a "He can." That's why God uses inadequate people—so He is glorified instead of us.

What do you struggle with? It might not be guilt, loneliness, and doubt for you, but it's definitely something. God uses our weakness to show us His great strength. Lean into it today.

———— ✳ ————

CHAPTER 13

START SMALL TODAY

✳

[God] says to ordinary people like me and you that instead of closing our eyes and bowing our heads, sometimes God wants us to keep our eyes open for people in need, do something about it, and bow our whole lives to Him instead.

BOB GOFF

WHEN MY YOUNGER DAUGHTER was four, she had a new friend over from preschool. Before they ran up to her room to pull out the Barbie dolls, Emerson gave her friend a quick tour of our home. I stood back and watched, delighted to see my little one act so big. I laughed when she pointed out obvious things like the chairs and table. She showed her guest the bathroom and laundry room, and when she got to the kitchen, she ran over to the photographs of brown faces covering our refrigerator. The friend looked confused.

"Who are those people?"

"These are the people we help in Africa," she said matter-of-factly. "What does your family do?"

It wasn't so much what she said that took my breath away—it

was the way she said it. Confident. Knowing. I smiled at her simple faith. She had every reason to believe that all families do their one thing for God. She didn't miss a beat, moving on to the snack basket in the pantry.

If I could give my children anything in this life, it would be this piece of wisdom: doing good work for Jesus doesn't make us special or extraordinary; it shows we're Christians. And it's the one gift I pray you take from my story.

Because if you've read this far, you've realized we are ordinary and a lot like you.

I knew I needed to write this book the day a mom from church rang my doorbell. When I opened the door, she was standing on the porch with several garbage bags. "I hope you don't mind my dropping by," she said, "but I wanted to give these things to you for Mercy House." I gladly accepted her generous gifts of baby clothes, toys, and accessories.

And then she said the words I hear nearly every time I speak to a mom about this God-sized dream. "I really want to support what you're doing. It's so inspiring! But I could never do anything like that. I'm just a mom."

When I heard those words, I wanted to say, "*I'm just a mom too.*" I desperately wanted to point out the piles of laundry, to show her the dirty floors and mounds of dust bunnies that multiply, well, like rabbits. I wanted to confess that I hadn't started dinner yet and I had no idea what I was making. If I had invited her into the house, she would have seen one child in a time-out and another one rolling her eyes at me. I wanted this mom to know that God didn't wait for me to get my life together before I said yes—He accepted my willingness in the middle of my mess. I wanted to sit down and tell her the broken pieces of my story—not to receive glory, but to show her His glory.

I wanted to blast these words into the sky:

Dear moms, love God; love others. It's a simple response to His great love for us. You don't have to do something big for Him; just do something because your yes matters! He can make something beautiful from your life too.

Why do we believe we aren't good enough or smart enough or just plain *enough* to do something for God? We moms multi-task, whip up gourmet dinners from three ingredients, stretch a dollar a mile, rock a baby on our hip while we wipe another one's bottom; we birth people and raise them into amazing adults! But when it comes to Kingdom business, we believe the lie that we can't do significant things for God. Being a mother *is* a significant thing we can do for the Kingdom. Raising children to love Jesus and honor others is changing the world.

I received this e-mail from one of my blog followers. Her name is Hannah and she's a mom. And she was about to show me how God works.

Hi, Kristen:

As a cloth-diapering mama myself, I noticed on your "Mercy House wish list" page that you need plastic sofa covers because "cloth diapered babies leak."

They shouldn't!

I have an idea for you. There are many, many cloth diaper manufacturers now and two of my personal

*favorites (for their business ethic and faith-based company
models) are Cotton Babies (one of the largest in the
business) and Lovely Pocket Diapers (a smaller, WAHM
[Work at Home Moms] operation). I was thinking
that perhaps you could contact them for donations or
for reduced costs for a bulk order for your Mercy House
babies. Cotton Babies already has a system in place for
those in need. . . . I know they even offer hefty discounts
for missionary/pastoral families, because my friends who
are serving in east Asia received a full stash of Econobums
(their prefold line) for a very low price.*

    *Anyway, just an idea I had while looking down your
list!*

    Bless you, sister!

Hannah

I'm a full-time blogger/writer and run a nonprofit from home,
and I get hundreds of e-mails a week. I try to respond to personal
e-mails like this so I sent Hannah a quick response that said,

    *Great idea! Everything we use has been donated and is
used. I don't have time to ask for donations, but maybe
I can find someone who does.*

    Blessings.

Kristen

Well. Two days later, I received two different e-mails/phone
calls from CEOs of diaper companies wanting to donate thousands of dollars in cloth diapers, covers, and accessories! I was
floored. I dug the e-mail from Hannah out of my inbox and

asked her what she wrote to these companies. She sent me one of the e-mails to share with you:

Dear Cotton Babies:

I've loved our Cotton Babies diapers for the past couple years. Our entire stash consists of your terrific bumGenius Elementals and 4.0s, thanks to the generosity of friends at our baby showers. Nearly all my good friends from college cloth diaper and they use Cotton Babies diapers as well; you have a terrific reputation in my circle of friends! I talk about you all the time, especially when a new mama is interested in exploring the world of cloth diapering.

I also appreciate your exemplary customer service. Your reps were always incredibly helpful when, as a new mother, I called with "desperate" questions about cloth diapering!

I want to share a story with you. I grew up as a third-culture kid in western Africa, in the developing nation of Cameroon. Most people haven't heard of it—unless they're soccer fans! Anyway, I grew up seeing a lot of extreme poverty. Also, my husband served in the navy for several years, and one of the most poignant memories he has (and part of what brought him to Christ) was working with Somalian refugees and assisting with building projects in Djibouti. Hence, our hearts are always tender toward Africa.

Are you familiar with We Are THAT Family? Kristen and Maureen (and their friends and family) work very hard to run Mercy House, a home in Kenya for young, single mothers and their babies, a place to offer a sanctuary and peace for these women and babies in desperate situations, a place where they can learn marketable crafts as well as about Jesus, who loves them more than anything.

Recently, I was reading through their "needs" list, and something caught my eye. They said they needed plastic couch covers, because "cloth diapers leak"! I thought, "No, no, no! They shouldn't have to cover their couches with plastic because they have diapers in poor condition!" I contacted Kristen about reaching out to some cloth diaper manufacturers on their behalf. So here I am.

I thought of you first because, frankly, Cotton Babies' business ethic and faith have impressed and inspired me over the past couple of years as I've been cloth-diapering my little guy. I know that you offer Econobums at a greatly reduced cost to missionaries and pastoral families (some of my friends serving in Southeast Asia have been blessed by your generosity). Mercy House, unfortunately, doesn't have the funds to afford even that.

Would you consider partnering with Mercy House in doing the Lord's work of providing for these beautiful women and their precious babies and, specifically, donating diapers to them?

Thank you for taking the time to read this. I very much appreciate it!

Blessings to you,

Hannah G.

This one mom who spends a lot of her time wiping bums and changing diapers is changing the world through diapers! She sent one e-mail about something she's passionate about and got thousands of dollars in diapers donated. Her small yes was the catalyst to meet a huge need across the ocean. She is just one of countless moms who have helped build and maintain Mercy House one yes at a time.

Here's the thing: I couldn't do Mercy House by myself—and I don't! Together we are the body of Christ.

The body is a unit, though it is made up of many parts; and though all its parts are many, they form one body. So it is with Christ. For we were all baptized by one Spirit into one body—whether Jews or Greeks, slave or free—and we were all given the one Spirit to drink.

Now the body is not made up of one part but of many. If the foot should say, "Because I am not a hand, I do not belong to the body," it would not for that reason cease to be part of the body. And if the ear should say, "Because I am not an eye, I do not belong to the body," it would not for that reason cease to be part of the body. If the whole body were an eye, where would the sense of hearing be? If the whole body were an ear, where would the sense of smell be? But in fact God has arranged the parts in the body, every one of them, just as he wanted them to be. If they were all one part, where would the body be? As it is, there are many parts, but one body.

The eye cannot say to the hand, "I don't need you!" And the head cannot say to the feet, "I don't need you!" On the contrary, those parts of the body that seem to be weaker are indispensable, and the parts that we think are less honorable we treat with special honor. And the parts that are unpresentable are treated with special modesty, while our presentable parts need no special treatment. But God has combined the members of the body and has given greater honor to the parts that lacked it, so that there should be no division in the body, but that its parts should have equal concern for each other. If one part suffers, every part suffers with it; if one part is honored, every part rejoices with it.

I CORINTHIANS 12:12-26

Some of us are the hands, some are the feet, some are the bums. By myself I would have had just an idea, Maureen would have had willingness, Suzanne (who takes all our pictures and has become my right-hand person in the States) would have had just her camera, and Hannah would have had a lot of diapers. But together, along with so many others, we have all said yes in our own unique ways to create something substantial and powerful that is changing lives and bringing glory to Jesus.

We rejoice together as a whole because one small part is vital to the health of the body. Diapers might not seem like a big deal to you, but this one part meets a real need for my Kenyan mothers. My husband calls it the domino effect. God strategically placed people in our lives, church, and all over the world who were willing to go with us on this journey of starting something from nothing. Most of what I thought would happen didn't. Most of the people I thought would help haven't. But God has provided the right people at exactly the right time because His plans are so much better than mine.

Our maternity home in Kenya has more than a dozen teen mommas now, each with a baby. In the summer of 2013, we paid cash (nearly $200,000) for our first permanent home, with the plan to buy another one in the spring of 2014 and then begin to reach outside our residential homes to the young single moms living in the slums. All that has happened because in 2013, our second full year of operation, a "bunch of moms" gave nearly half a million dollars.

We have helped girls from unthinkable situations—unimaginable poverty, horrific abuse, orphaned girls without another soul in the world to love them. We have watched them heal, slowly and beautifully transforming into women of God. We have stepped into a crisis and said, "Jesus loves you" the best way we know how.

These girls now carry big dreams of becoming doctors, teachers, policewomen, and newscasters. We are helping their families start businesses (because this ultimately helps our girls), and we are training them to disciple others once they graduate. Mercy House is full of healthy (yes, fat) babies and toddlers who would not otherwise be alive today. This home exists in a faraway country because a bunch of mothers said yes in their own small way.

❋

When I said good-bye to our Rehema House family and Maureen at the end of my trip in the spring of 2013, it was with more peace and joy than I thought possible. Usually, leaving is hard. There are tears and doubts, and I always feel like I'm leaving Maureen with the hardest job in the world. But something very special happened toward the end of that week.

While Maureen and I were in downtown Nairobi shopping for fabric samples for the skills program, her phone rang. She answered, then whispered, "It's for you," and handed it to me. It was Oliver, Maureen's boyfriend, whom our family had met on an earlier trip. Maureen and Oliver had met as children and had gone through Compassion's Leadership Development program together. We liked Oliver's soft-spoken nature and quiet strength. Oliver works as a social worker at one of Kenya's only adoption agencies.

"Mom Kristen?" Oliver said nervously over the phone. "I want to ask Maureen to marry me while you are here." I tried not to gasp. I had to pretend like he was asking me something totally different. It was so hard to act normal when I wanted to jump up and down. I can't recount how many Skype conversations Maureen and I had had about her desire and need for a husband to share her life with.

Oliver proposing

Later that day, Oliver brought Maureen's mom to the home for a sewing class, and the timing was perfect. With all the residents sitting down for "a meeting" and with Maureen's family there, Oliver got down on one knee and proposed. Maureen was shocked! I cried when she said yes. It was beautiful seeing her experience one of life's greatest pleasures in front of the residents who dreamed of the same moment in their lives one day.

I left Kenya with a happy heart.

I had been home from Kenya for about a month when I got an urgent message from Maureen. Her sweet mother, Jennifer, whom our family had fallen in love with on several of our visits, had been diagnosed with a brain tumor. It was the news we feared most after watching her struggle with her eyesight and eventually become blind in one eye. I knew this new crisis would be hard to overcome. Maureen had been through so much loss in the short three years I had known her, with the deaths of her sister and nephew. When I read Jennifer's doctor's report, I realized this tumor was a matter of life and death. I knew we had to do something.

Because if I have learned anything from this journey, it is this: one life is worth fighting for.

This was personal. It wasn't a random face in Africa who needed life-saving surgery. It was someone I loved. She was the mother of people I loved. Her life had a wonderful impact on our home in Kenya, where she volunteered, and she was a strong tower to Maureen. Jennifer was seen as the grandmother to our residents and their babies. She would come in her quiet, peaceful way and hold babies and encourage mommas. On several occasions, her motherly instinct provided wisdom that ended up protecting our babies. One of those times, Maureen was visit-

ing me in America and Jennifer was dropping in on the staff and residents to check on them occasionally. One day, she got there and saw that several of the babies were ill and getting worse quickly. Without hesitating, she insisted the staff take them to the hospital, and doctors commended her fast thinking. I simply couldn't fathom what losing

Jennifer

her would mean, and so I didn't. I shifted into fight mode.

And by fight mode, what I really mean is I cried and struggled and complained to God, especially after learning the surgery would cost $25,000. In my world, that is a significant amount of money. We had recently purchased the home in Kenya for Mercy House, and I was coming off a fund-raising sprint. I knew I couldn't raise money through our organization for Maureen's mom because it didn't fit into the parameters of our vision statement. Plus, to be totally honest, I was tired. Tired of being the woman who always asked for money.

I brainstormed, e-mailed, took notes, and begged God to help us fund this surgery to save Jennifer. And then a week before the scheduled surgery, pieces began to fall into place. We found an organization (CURE Kenya) that would allow us to raise funds through them, and the hospital (where all twelve of our babies at the time had been delivered) decided to reduce the cost of Jennifer's surgery by half because of the good work Maureen was doing through Mercy House.

God was moving and suddenly $12,500 didn't seem like a big deal at all. It certainly wasn't for God. I wrote about it on my blog, and donations began to pour in from mommas (and daddies) around the world to help a woman they had never met. They joined the fight to save Jennifer, and in less than thirty-six hours the body of Christ raised $15,000. I watched God's arithmetic in action: taking small offerings from big hearts and multiplying them miraculously.

Jennifer thanked everyone who helped.

Dear friends and extended families,

I greet you in the mighty name of Jesus, hoping that you are well.

I want to thank God in a very special way for having done me a miracle. When I started treatment, the doctors were talking of a big amount of money. I was asking myself where the money would come from since Maureen is the only one earning in our family.

One evening I received a call from Maureen telling me, "Mom, guess what? The money for the hospital bill has been raised all within two days." I was shocked and confused, and the only words that came out of my mouth were "Thank You, Jesus, for the love and favor You have for me."

I want to thank my sister Kristen in every special way for having mobilized people who don't know me to do the fundraising. The heart and favor you have is not with many. My next thanks goes to all who contributed and those who participated in one way or another. May the almighty God bless you abundantly.

I cannot forget to thank CURE for permitting Kristen to raise funds for my hospital bill. May God bless you.

I am kindly asking you to pray for me.

God bless you.

✳

A. W. Tozer wrote, "God rescues us by breaking us, by shattering our strength and wiping out our resistance."[1] Are you ready to be broken for Him? I know for a fact that He works things out for our good and rescues us when we don't even know we are lost. And if we are obedient to Him, miracles can happen.

Start today, right where you are. I'm not trying to oversimplify or dodge the issue. I don't know what your yes will look like, but I can guarantee that there are opportunities in your life today to say it.

Look for the yes in these areas.

Yourself. The best place to start is by looking in the mirror. Ask yourself how you can get emotionally, physically, and spiritually healthier today. Do you need to forgive or ask forgiveness? Do you need to take time for yourself? Do you need to dream again? Take some time right now and have a heart-to-heart talk with God. Lay down your burden and simply ask Jesus for an opportunity to say yes. And then watch out!

Often the best way to see the needs of others is to stop looking at our own. It's easy to get wrapped up in our own problems and have a skewed perspective. Looking up and out is a great way to help us see how much we have and be grateful. Even if you are experiencing lean times, give thanks, too—no matter what.

Motherhood. If you are a mom, acknowledge that everything you do for your child—yes, you, in the laundry room trying to get those stubborn stains out of her clothes—is service to our Lord. Motherhood is humbling. We can catch vomit like world-class athletes and we are marathon multitaskers. What you do every day for your children *matters*; start believing it.

> Offer grace to your kids when they least expect it but need it the most.
> Say yes as often as you can.
> Call another mother and ask her how she's really doing.
> Look for the God moments in the middle of your mess.

Marriage. Our relationship with our spouse needs constant maintenance. When we don't deal with issues or we ignore cracks in our marital foundation, it can build resentment and create devastating results. Here are some ways to give your marriage a boost:

> Serve your spouse in unexpected ways. Enjoy surprising him.
> Try not to speak negatively to your spouse for the next thirty days. Start now.
> Thank your spouse often—just because.

Ministry. Assess your role in full-time or parachurch ministry. You might not be in formal ministry, but everyone is called to do something for Jesus. Are you reading your Bible and praying regularly? Is there joy in your service? Are you neglecting your family or relationships with others in order to serve?

> Ask yourself if you're surviving or thriving. Be honest. Life's too short to just barely make it. God wants us to thrive.
> Make yourself rest if you feel burned out.
> Set aside a day to spend with God, praying, journaling, and listening to Him.
> Commit to a five-minute act of service for Jesus. It could be something as simple as sending an encouraging text, adding a few things to your grocery list for the local food pantry, or taking a package to the post office for a housebound acquaintance. Whatever it is, quietly pray and thank Him while serving.

Family. Mercy House is something we do as a family. My kids pitch in and help carry the burden. They pray for our girls in Kenya and rejoice with us when a new baby is born. There are pictures all over our house of their African family. This is our one thing. I am convinced that families who seize opportunities to say yes are stronger because of their common cause. Start by assessing the strength of your family.

Do you have regular family meals? Commit to changing that if you don't.

Incorporate a devotional time with your children and have them contribute to it.

Write a family mission statement.

Read inspiring books together. (You can find a list on my website: http://wearethatfamily.com/2012/05 /80-books-to-inspire-and-challenge-your-family.)

Serve together locally and globally. (See "100+ Ways for Your Family to Make a Difference" on my website: http://wearethatfamily.com/2011/06/100-ways-for -your-family-to-make-a-difference.)

Consumerism. We live in a consumer nation, and although it can seem overwhelming trying to navigate this area, we can start small and become more and more responsible.

Educate yourself on slave labor and check tags on products to see where they are manufactured. (The website www.shoptostopslavery.com has a lot of information.)

Buy fair-trade gifts to give and bless twice.

Support cause-related fashion (like Sevenly shirts, Freeset totes, Mercy House jewelry).

Generosity. Once we understand how much we have and compare ourselves to the world rather than to our peers, generosity finds its place in our hearts. I want to challenge you to give until it's just a little uncomfortable because comfortable generosity isn't really generosity. Scraping the cream off and offering it is easy. The kind of generosity that changes us is reaching deep and giving from that place. It's choosing to lay down some of our desires to help others with their needs. It's what makes us truly rich. Hold loosely to what's in your hand so that if you have the opportunity to give generously, you can.

> Sponsor one child or more through Compassion International or World Vision.
> See if your employer has a matching program for your financial gift.
> Give the money you've set aside for something frivolous to someone in need.

❊ ❀ ❊

UNPINNED FAITH

Saying yes isn't really about doing it all. It's about saying yes right where you are. It may seem small or insignificant, but any time you love someone or care for another person's needs, you're changing their world, and yours, too. It's about looking up from your everyday life and seeing opportunities around you to make a difference. It's about loving others as we are loved.

The apostle Peter reminded members of the early church of this in his first letter. "Be like-minded, be sympathetic, love one another, be compassionate and humble" (1 Peter 3:8).

✳

CHAPTER 14

WHAT REALLY HAPPENS WHEN WE MAKE JESUS ENOUGH

———— ✳ ————

There is no situation so chaotic that God cannot—from that situation—create something that is surpassingly good. He did it at creation. He did it at the cross. He is doing it today.

HANDLEY C. G. MOULE

IT'S BEEN FOUR YEARS since I stood on that filthy path in Mathare Valley and asked God how He could allow His people to suffer. It's the day He asked me the same thing.

It was the day I woke up.

I have never been the same. The smells, the sights, and the sorrow have been etched into my soul. And no matter where I go—from Disney World on a carefree family vacation to the amazing once-in-a-lifetime trip to Hawaii my husband won, the school carpool line, or a trip to Target—I carry the sorrow with me.

Oh, I laugh and do meaningless things; I am able to enjoy life and my children. But I cannot forget what happened to my heart. It broke. Shattered hearts heal, but they always bear scars so we won't forget the brokenness.

I asked God to break my heart with what broke His, and He did—over and over. Sometimes it looks like a hopeless pregnant girl in a slum or a dirty baby sitting on a pile of trash. Sometimes it's a brain tumor. Sometimes it's a heart attack or heartache.

And sometimes it's all of these at the same time.

What I didn't know when I stood on that dirty path was that it would lead to more joy and more meaning in my life than I could imagine. I've never felt more alive or more certain of what God wants me to do. The path has also led to sorrow I couldn't fathom—a deep, abiding awareness of the suffering in our world. I stand in the middle of joy and sorrow. That place is uncomfortable, and it forces me to depend on Jesus for every step.

One week after we raised $15,000 to save Jennifer's life, Maureen checked her mother into the Kenyan hospital that had lovingly cared for our Rehema House family. We understood the risks, but giving this precious fifty-three-year-old mother a chance at life sealed the decision. I was proud of those who had rallied and joined us to raise enough money for Jennifer's surgery. To be honest, I might have even patted myself on the back, thinking how she wouldn't have had a fighting chance at life without our efforts. Even waiting on word a world away, I never once doubted that God would perform another miracle, just as He had countless other times.

But sometimes God's plans don't make sense to us. God never promises us that He won't give us more than we can handle; He promises we won't be alone. Jennifer never recovered from her brain surgery. After five harrowing days in intensive care, she died. After five long, emotionally draining days with Maureen constantly at her side, she left this world.

During this ordeal, I had been constantly checking my e-mail, waiting on word of Jennifer's improvement. I was having a hard time sleeping on that fourth night, and I got up to see if there had been any change. And that's when I read Maureen's heartbreaking news. I called her immediately and prayed with her through our tears. There just wasn't anything else to do. I stumbled around my dark house for an hour, numbed by the news. I was lost. I had so many questions and swirling emotions. My heart was broken for Maureen and her young brothers, who were shocked by this devastating loss of their beautiful mother.

My house was quiet—kids sleeping, husband away on a business trip—and I lay prostrate on my closet floor and sobbed. I simply couldn't stand under the burden a second longer.

On that same phone call, Maureen told me our new home in Kenya had been broken into; our caretaker had been beaten and several items stolen. The next day two of our young mothers had C-sections scheduled, and as much as we wanted to rejoice with them, Mercy House was still reeling from loss on top of loss. Three days later, my father had a heart attack. With everyone looking to me to hold it all together, I was barely hanging on.

I gave up.

All week I'd been told by my concerned family and friends who were supporting us that we were in a spiritual battle as Jennifer fought for her life, just one more trial in what seemed like a never-ending onslaught. People reminded me how much the enemy hates the work of rescuing girls and saving babies. I believed it, but I have to say, some news makes you feel like you're losing the battle.

I knew God was in control, but things felt out of control.

And once again, it was painfully obvious I had no control. I wanted to close my eyes to the sorrow in this world. There have been times when I long to go back to being an oblivious mom whose biggest worry was redoing her home decor.

I was angry with God. In these short years that seemed to have lasted a lifetime, I'd come full circle, back to the point of shaking my fist in His face, crying, "How can You allow this?" Maureen's grief for her mother was so deep that I feared it would paralyze the good work we were doing in Kenya. "I am tired of suffering and sorrow. How can it be possible for You to receive glory through this? If I had known this would be the outcome, I never would have raised the money for Jennifer's surgery."

God didn't make sense to me.

I knew we were in a fierce, unseen battle. I e-mailed the Mercy House board members with the latest news of Jennifer's death and the other events of the week and begged for their prayers. This response from our godly Russian friend Sasha spoke to me:

> *You are not going to lose the battle because it was already WON on the Cross. I don't believe in losing or getting the victories because Jesus has already done it. The question is, how far will you go to declare the victory in this battle? Would two more rescued girls make you know it? Or two thousand more? How far will you go to proclaim that the victory was DONE for you?*
>
> *No, this battle is never going to be easy. It is only the beginning of the hardship. But if you choose to endure with Him, you choose to reign with Him. If you choose to suffer, you will be glorified.*

The moment you think you have no more energy to go on is exactly when you will experience the supernatural power of Christ working in you and through you. His power is not for backup, after you've tried to do it on your own. Once you have given your life to Christ, everything you do is by Him, through Him, and with Him. It was the same power that the apostle Paul relied upon:

As God's partners, we beg you not to accept this marvelous gift of God's kindness and then ignore it. For God says,

> *"At just the right time, I heard you.*
> *On the day of salvation, I helped you."*

Indeed, the "right time" is now. Today is the day of salvation.

We live in such a way that no one will stumble because of us, and no one will find fault with our ministry. In everything we do, we show that we are true ministers of God. We patiently endure troubles and hardships and calamities of every kind. We have been beaten, been put in prison, faced angry mobs, worked to exhaustion, endured sleepless nights, and gone without food. We prove ourselves by our purity, our understanding, our patience, our kindness, by the Holy Spirit within us, and by our sincere love. We faithfully preach the truth. God's power is working in us. We use the weapons of righteousness in the right hand for attack and the left hand for defense. We serve God whether people honor us or despise us, whether

> *they slander us or praise us. We are honest, but they call*
> *us impostors. We are ignored, even though we are well*
> *known. We live close to death, but we are still alive. We*
> *have been beaten, but we have not been killed. Our*
> *hearts ache, but we always have joy. We are poor, but*
> *we give spiritual riches to others. We own nothing, and*
> *yet we have everything.* 2 CORINTHIANS 6:1-10, NLT

Paul's words were a gentle but forceful reminder that this is
the gospel: hardships, trials, and persecution—even death.

I have to tell you the truth: making Jesus enough is hard,
sorrowful work. It's not pretty. It doesn't make a happy greeting
card or inspire a cute saying on a mug. It won't make you rich
or popular. It doesn't sell books or fill auditoriums. This is not
the Christianity in America we hear from televangelists. It's ugly
and dirty work. It's a gut-wrenching, soul-splitting journey, and
it comes at a high cost.

And yet when the doubts begin to creep in, His sovereignty
reaches into our doubt and says "I AM. Everything else will fade
because I am eternal."

In the weeks following the heartbreak about Jennifer, I began
to see the world as Jesus sees it.

In Matthew 9:36, when Jesus looked out on the crowd of
people, He didn't just love them—He was moved with compassion for them. The word *compassion* in this text actually means
"to suffer with." He looked past their faces and saw their needs,
and He suffered with them.

Making Jesus enough in your life opens your eyes to the way
He sees the world. And it changes you.

My mind flashed back to a five-by-seven-foot shanty in

the middle of the hellish garbage dump, the hovel that young Vincent called home. The entire time we were together he had exuded so much peace and joy that I finally asked him, "Why are you so happy? Why aren't you afraid?"

"Because I have Jesus."

You are so wise, Vincent. I understand it now. Jesus is enough.

As I cried for Maureen and her family, I clung to these words from someone who knew what constant suffering was like:

For what we preach is not ourselves, but Jesus Christ as Lord, and ourselves as your servants for Jesus' sake. For God, who said, "Let light shine out of darkness," made his light shine in our hearts to give us the light of the knowledge of God's glory displayed in the face of Christ.

But we have this treasure in jars of clay to show that this all-surpassing power is from God and not from us. We are hard pressed on every side, but not crushed; perplexed, but not in despair; persecuted, but not abandoned; struck down, but not destroyed. We always carry around in our body the death of Jesus, so that the life of Jesus may also be revealed in our body. For we who are alive are always being given over to death for Jesus' sake, so that his life may also be revealed in our mortal body. So then, death is at work in us, but life is at work in you. . . .

Therefore we do not lose heart. Though outwardly we are wasting away, yet inwardly we are being renewed day by day. For our light and momentary troubles are achieving for us an eternal glory that far outweighs them

all. So we fix our eyes not on what is seen, but on what
is unseen, since what is seen is temporary, but what is
unseen is eternal. 2 CORINTHIANS 4:5-12, 16-18

I let Jesus be enough because He is. He held my fragile clay
jar together. The darkness in our lives only makes Jesus shine
brighter. The victory is His.

Don't be afraid, for I am with you.
    Don't be discouraged, for I am your God.
I will strengthen you and help you.
    I will hold you up with my victorious right hand.
ISAIAH 41:10, NLT

We are created for two reasons: to fellowship with God and
to bring Him glory.
I want to do both.
Even when neither makes sense.

For days after Jennifer's death, I walked around in a fog. I
didn't know what to do, a condition I was all too familiar with.
I wanted to jump on a plane and fly to Kenya and fix things.
But I couldn't fix this. It was beyond my control; I would only
add confusion to chaos and possibly make matters worse in my
effort to help.

Instead I waited and prayed. I watched God begin to send
the right people to stand in the gap so Maureen could take time
off to grieve with her younger brothers. I watched God provide
more money for a funeral and provide the first steps of healing.
From afar, I watched a broken, devastated Maureen praise Jesus
in the lowest days of her life.

I watched Him receive glory in an unthinkable situation.

❋

At the end of that first Compassion International blogging trip, the team of bloggers took some time to decompress and talk about reentry into our world back home. We were all sort of numb and emotional from the past week. I immediately thought about the night before I left when my church had prayed over me. As I sat in the pew, terrified of the unknown, I turned in my Bible to Isaiah 58:7-9. The words burrowed deep into my heart. I closed my eyes while others around me were singing, and I prayed, "God, this is my prayer. Give me an opportunity to live this. Amen." It felt like a personal message just for me. It still does.

> What I'm interested in seeing you do is:
>> sharing your food with the hungry,
>> inviting the homeless poor into your homes,
>> putting clothes on the shivering ill-clad,
>> being available to your own families.
> Do this and the lights will turn on,
>> and your lives will turn around at once.
> Your righteousness will pave your way.
>> The God of glory will secure your passage.
> Then when you pray, God will answer.
>> You'll call out for help and I'll say, "Here I am."
>> (*The Message*)

Shaun Groves, our Compassion trip leader, cautiously warned us about rushing into big decisions too quickly, about how it would feel to return to our lives, about the need to tread carefully on our expectations of others. He reminded us of where we were before our trip and how everyone's response looks different.

"You will respond," he warned. "Doing nothing is as much a response as doing something." In the moonlight that night, none of us knew what our response would look like.

Never in a million years would I have dreamed that I would go home and start a nonprofit within six months of hearing those words. I still don't see myself as someone who fits that bill; I cringe every time I see the title "president" after my name. But these words in 1 John 3:16-17 propel me to put one foot in front of the other.

> This is how we've come to understand and experience
> love: Christ sacrificed his life for us. This is why we
> ought to live sacrificially for our fellow believers, and
> not just be out for ourselves. If you see some brother
> or sister in need and have the means to do something
> about it but turn a cold shoulder and do nothing, what
> happens to God's love? It disappears. And you made it
> disappear. (*The Message*)

After church one Sunday, Terrell texted me this thought that sums up our awakening:

> The American Dream would not be our dream if we
> could catch a glimpse of how much greater God's dreams
> are for us. Placed next to the enormity of God's plans
> for us, the American Dream seems utterly absurd in its
> smallness.

If the apostle Paul were texting, it would read exactly like Philippians 3:8-9:

Yes, all the things I once thought were so important are gone from my life. Compared to the high privilege of knowing Christ Jesus as my Master, firsthand, everything I once thought I had going for me is insignificant—dog dung. I've dumped it all in the trash so that I could embrace Christ and be embraced by him. I didn't want some petty, inferior brand of righteousness that comes from keeping a list of rules when I could get the robust kind that comes from trusting Christ—*God's* righteousness. (*The Message*)

I still have more questions than answers. I am still uncertain and I still need Jesus. But that's exactly how He wants my fragile clay jar to be—full of Him, not me. He does what we cannot so it's clear to the world that He is the one to be glorified. Salvation is not riding on our performance; it's riding on His strength.

Most of all, making Jesus enough in my life makes me long for heaven. I am filled with the blessed hope that one day sorrow will end, that death will be swallowed up. He will wipe away our tears, and suffering will cease. I long for more of Him, to be with my Savior for eternity. Until that happens, I am living my life with my eyes open.

UNPINNED FAITH

I don't know what your response will look like after reading this book; you probably don't either. But you will respond. Don't ever forget that one simple yes can be a catalyst for God to do what we've never seen done before.

Making Jesus enough isn't about good works or being good enough. It's about peeling back all the layers, the blessings, the stuff in our hearts, and discovering our desperate need for Him. When we remove the extras, we find we are not enough. And we see that He is.

When you make Jesus enough, *He becomes all you need.*

KENYA, WINTER 2013

❋

What is joy without sorrow? What is success without failure?
What is a win without a loss? What is health without illness?
You have to experience each if you are to appreciate the other.
There is always going to be suffering. It's how you look at your suffering,
how you deal with it, that will define you.

MARK TWAIN

AFTER JENNIFER'S UNEXPECTED DEATH, just two months after Maureen's engagement and five months before her November 2013 wedding day, it was a dark season of grief.

How do you encourage someone who has lost so much? I simply didn't have words of encouragement. I prayed that the Holy Spirit would comfort Maureen. She continued working and pouring her heart into Rehema House, but her joy was gone. I continued to tell the story of what God was doing in Kenya and to raise money, but I was filled with worry for this girl I loved so far away.

We kept moving—slowly—putting one foot in front of the other.

I remember the day I whispered to Terrell, "Maureen is going to be okay." It was the day she asked me via Skype to help her find turquoise wedding satin for the bridesmaids' dresses and for the groomsmen's bow ties and cummerbunds. She was still mourning, *but she remembered it was okay to keep living.* I bought fifty yards of fabric, and my family moved all the furniture in the living room to create space so we could fold the six-foot length of material until it was small enough to fit into a suitcase.

Traveling to Kenya as a family is not only expensive, it's exhausting, and traveling to Kenya during the week of Thanksgiving in the middle of the busy holiday season is even harder. One day over Skype, Maureen said that if we were able to come, she'd love for all three of my kids to be in the wedding . . . and for me to stand in as mother of the bride. More than ever, I wanted to be there when she walked down the aisle. I knew I could never replace Jennifer. But I'm a mom and all I really know how to do is love.

In July, our twelfth baby was born, and the new home in Kenya was at capacity. The parents or guardians (we try to identify a supportive adult in all of the Rehema House mothers' lives) of the residents had started small-business training. We were also making some challenging decisions about education, and three of the residents had started the slow process of reintegration, which includes home visits with a social worker in hopes of eventually bringing the families back together.

Education is important in Kenya. With an unemployment rate of 44 percent, people need at least an eighth-grade education in order to have any chance at employment. In Kenya, girls who become pregnant lose this opportunity and fall behind. We started planning the first Rehema House graduation, where residents would move from phase one, which included education in the home, to phase two, which allowed for more independence and education at a local day school. I selfishly suggested that the graduation take place the same week as Maureen's wedding. I knew it was our best shot at being in Kenya for both monumental events. Maureen agreed.

We arrived in Kenya at 7 a.m. on the Monday before Thanksgiving after nearly two days of travel (note to self: cheap international airline tickets are cheap for a reason—they add an extra twelve hours to an already long twenty-four hours of travel). Instead of finding beds and crashing, we went straight to the house where twelve girls and their babies were waiting to greet us. Reunited! We spent the next couple of days recording videos and documenting their lives in pictures as testimonies to what God had done. We were so happy that the toddlers were eager to play with us and that there were new babies to meet and hold. Giggles filled the house.

"Would you like to hold Eugene?" Rose, one of the girls, asked me. I took her precious son, bundled up in a blue blanket, and held him close. She was so proud.

"He's beautiful," I whispered. She knelt on one side of the bed; I was on the other. We grasped hands for a second, and in the moment, without words, we spoke love and hope.

It was hard not to notice the cramped living space for our twenty-four residents and all the staff of the organization, all under one roof. There wasn't one empty bed for a mother or a baby. It was confirmation that we needed to continue to raise money for a second home.

On the third day of our trip, we traveled to a local church for the graduation. The graduating girls will be moving out of the house and into either a nearby rented home with a housemother or into the second home we hope to purchase in 2014. While they

Celebrating after the graduation ceremony

are still under the care of Rehema, they will gain more independence and visit home more often. As I looked at Charity, Cindy, Quinter, and Sarah, my eyes filled with tears. These girls who had once cowered and acted out, who had cried every day and lived with a survivor mentality, now stood tall and proud. The graduates wore purple caps and gowns to symbolize their royalty as daughters of the King of kings. They sang with confidence and danced with pride. They held their toddlers by the hands; they were a living testimony to the miraculous hand of God.

I briefly shared how Rehema House began, and Terrell charged the girls with Scripture. He also empowered them with these words:

I charge you to be women of God. Women of integrity. Women of faith.

I charge you to both study and live out the Word of God.

I charge you to raise your children to be followers of Christ.

I charge you to be faithful like Rahab, even though you may have to go against what others think you should do.

I charge you, like Ruth, to forsake everything, to make right choices and follow Christ.

I charge you, as Mordecai charged Esther, to take hold of the grace of God in your life for such a time as this.

I charge you, like Mary, to be armed with an attitude that says, "Lord, let it be to me according to your word."

We knelt before these beautiful girls, along with Maureen, and we washed their feet. As I poured water over Cindy's feet and gently rubbed them with my hands, I understood what Mary must have felt when she cried onto the feet of Jesus. It was humbling to be on this holy ground.

We feasted with family and friends on Kenyan cuisine and then we got very sick. Our family spent the fourth day of our trip—Thanksgiving Day—with food poisoning, the kind that happens when foreign food is prepared in a way American stomachs can't handle. We gave thanks for medicine and chicken broth and felt much better the next day. Our trip was filled with hours (and hours) of traffic, exhaustion, sleep deprivation, slow Internet, and sickness. But those hardships were defeated by the sheer joy and peace that comes from following God where He leads. He gives us grace to take the next step. And even better, He goes with us, and *before* us, because He knows exactly what we are going to face and just how much we will need Him.

※

I think it's a universal given that weddings are stressful, no matter the size or location. Maureen had a lot on her to-do list leading up to her wedding, but I think she managed to accomplish it all. During her visit to America earlier in the year, we had secretly shopped for a wedding dress, veil, and shoes, courtesy of a very generous friend from church. Another friend made her a bouquet of silk flowers with a tiny picture of Maureen's mother attached to the stem, and I brought it with me, along with some artificial bouquets for the bridesmaids. Our family arrived at the church early, an hour before the 10:30 a.m. ceremony, but we waited an hour for Maureen to arrive (no one's in a hurry in Kenya). When the car pulled up, a mob of people dressed in tribal garb surrounded the car and danced, chanted, and sang for twenty minutes, with Maureen smiling from ear to ear inside the car, loving every minute of it. At one point, I leaned over with eyes as big as saucers and said to Terrell, "Our kids

Oliver and Maureen's wedding day

will never forget this." I caught my kids' eyes in the crowd and we all smiled at each other in wonder.

Terrell looked bewildered. "*I'll* never forget it!"

Kenyans know how to celebrate. And what a celebration! When Maureen, in brilliant white, walked down the aisle toward Oliver, the crowd hushed. She was stunning. Angelic. It was a beautiful ceremony and thankfully the

shortest part of the day because the honorary mother of the bride was trying to keep the flower girl and ring bearer, the firstborn Rehema babies who were now over two years old, occupied. I fed them Tic Tacs the entire time and they kept spitting them out in my hand. At one point, I motioned to Terrell, who was sitting behind me, and to Suzanne, who was taking pictures, that I needed food reinforcements. They passed me a can of Pringles. Travis, Charity's son, who was sitting in my lap in the front row, licked the salt off each chip and passed it down the row.

After the ceremony and pictures, we went to the reception. There were hundreds of people dancing; the rest of the guests were eating under tents. It was the largest wedding I've ever been to. I tried to find a quiet place to eat the canned chicken salad and crackers we had brought (our stomachs were still recovering), when I heard my name being called by the emcee. He was inviting my family to the center of the crowd.

To dance to two songs from both Maureen and Oliver's respective tribes.

I'm pretty sure there are people in Kenya still laughing about what they saw that day. But what happens in Africa stays in Africa.

The smile on Maureen's face on her wedding day will stay with me forever. She exuded happiness. I know she missed her mom. Maureen has tasted more sorrow and experienced more suffering than anyone I've ever known. To watch her experience the blessing of true love and marriage was a gift from God. Sorrow and joy, mingled. *"You have to experience each if you are to appreciate the other."*

❋

At the end of our trip, after the last budget meeting, I found a quiet place (which was challenging, with so many of us staying in Maureen's apartment) and I cried. I saw the big number at the bottom of the page: the funds needed for the next year to purchase another home, furnish it, bring in six more girls, provide maternity care and education, and begin replicating the residential program in the slums, helping young single moms, and so much more. I was filled with doubt. The size and responsibility of this yes was only growing, and I was afraid. Terrell was feeling overwhelmed with the weight of it too.

We didn't have a chance to talk about it because it was time to pack and head to the airport.

When we got to Paris for a layover, I turned my phone off since I didn't have Internet or good cell coverage. I was exhausted.

Unbeknownst to me, on the other side of the world, generous hearts were being mobilized by my friend Ann at (in)Courage, a branch of DaySpring. She and a team of (in)mercy bloggers were making people aware of Mercy House's need for $50,000 toward a second home in Kenya. In less than forty-eight hours, the goal was reached—and exceeded. When I turned on my phone the next day, I expected to see a few e-mails, but instead there were hundreds of e-mails and Tweets and messages from all over the world in witness of what God had provided.

I couldn't believe it! I let out a scream and shared the incredible news with my family. And yet I wasn't surprised a bit. It

Twelve girls, twelve babies. One yes.

was just like God to do the impossible in such an astounding way. It was not only supernatural; it was a clear message to me from God. He reminded me again that I wasn't alone and that He would do the impossible.

He continues to show me how He can take a small yes and make it enough.

My faith has been forged in fire. It may not be as sparkly as a rhinestone pin.

But it is real. And it shines.

ACKNOWLEDGMENTS

I think this is the hardest part to write because so many people have been a part of this journey.

First, to Terrell: You are the quiet, constant strength leading our home. You believed in this book long before I did, and I thank God for the way you love me. Our marriage and our lives are a testimony that Jesus makes everything beautiful. I can't wait to live the rest of the story with you. I love you with all my heart.

To my children: You are and will always be my greatest accomplishment. You teach me humility and grace, a lot about God and even more about myself. I love you deeply. The three of you are going to rock the world for Jesus!

To Maureen: I love the way God has woven our stories together. Thank you for letting me tell this one. Knowing you has made me a better person. I am stronger because I walked through the valley of the shadow of death with you. You inspire me to keep saying yes. I love you.

To the Rehema House family: Girls and babies, you are the heroes of this story. You've taught me and countless others to live courageously. You are a constant reminder that God takes the ashes of our lives and turns them into beauty. And to the board of directors: thank you for your yes!

To Mom and Dad: No one will ever know what a constant source of strength your unrelenting, unshakable support has been to our family as we've chased this crazy dream. Thank you for saying yes with us.

To my extended family: My in-laws and my sister, thank you for loving us through this journey and not saying we were crazy (even if you might have thought it). And to my precious sister-in-law in heaven, "favaunt," I can't wait to see you again. This is how Rhonda always signed her comments on my blog. It's an inside family joke

To my agent, Bill: You pulled this book out of me. Thank you for believing in this story and for helping me tell it.

To Ann: You are a gift to me. You have prayed when I couldn't. You have cried with me when I couldn't stop. Your steady voice over Voxer and in your writing has been God's voice to me so many times. I can't wait to get our hands dirty together and kneel down low for His glory.

To Team Mercy, the board of directors and volunteers: The quiet, hard work you do on behalf of these girls is Kingdom work. Suzanne, thank you for your friendship, your amazing pictures, your honesty. Karen, Carol, Mike and Lindsay, Jamie, Jen, and Ashley, you have been a part of this story since the beginning. Thank you for your faithfulness. It changes the world. And to the countless volunteers who serve, thank you!

To my blog readers and donors: You've become my community these past few years, and you believed in a dream that didn't exist, which really means you believed in me. Thank you for saying yes with me.

To the (in)Courage girls and Dayspring family: I trust you. Thank you for being a part of my life, for helping me pick out book cover colors and brainstorm ideas and mostly for supporting this God-sized dream.

To the Tyndale House family: Sarah, thank you for protecting this story and for letting me put the picture of my doll in this book. Bonne, you asked the hard questions and gave me the courage to answer them. Sharon, I felt your prayers throughout this entire process. Jennifer, you nailed the cover design! And to the entire marketing team, thank you for loving this story as much as I do.

NOTES

CHAPTER 3: FINDING BEAUTY IN THE BROKEN PIECES
1. Rick Warren, *The Purpose Driven Life* (Grand Rapids: Zondervan, 2002), 194.
2. Brad Price, *Romans Bible Commentary: Living By Faith* (Brad Price, publisher: 2005), 74–75, http://www.abiblecommentary.com/romanschapterthree.pdf.

CHAPTER 4: THE SWEET SPOT
1. Quoted in Tian Dayton, *Journey through Womanhood: Meditations from Our Collective Soul* (Center City, MN: Hazelden, 2002), 220.
2. Ann Voskamp, "How to Make a Miracle Happen," *A Holy Experience* (blog), February 22, 2013, http://www.aholyexperience.com/2013/02/how-to-make-a-miracle-happen.
3. John Piper, *Desiring God: Meditations of a Christian Hedonist* (Colorado Springs: Multnomah, 2011), 309.
4. Holley Gerth, *You're Made for a God-Sized Dream* (Grand Rapids: Revell, 2013), 51.
5. John Piper, *A Sweet and Bitter Providence: Sex, Race, and the Sovereignty of God* (Wheaton, IL: Crossway Books, 2009), 101–102.
6. Beth Moore, "What Would You Look Like?," *The Living Proof Ministries Blog*, March 26, 2013, http://blog.lproof.org/2013/03/what-would-you-look-like.html.

CHAPTER 6: GIVING BIRTH TO A DREAM
1. David McKenzie, "In Kenya, Few Choices to Backstreet Abortions," *CNN World*, March 24, 2010, http://www.cnn.com/2010/WORLD/africa/03/23/kenya.abortions.

CHAPTER 8: THAT MESSY PEACH PIE
1. Robert Brault, "Thoughts of Hope and Rejuvenation," *A Robert Brault Reader* (blog), May 1, 2009, http://www.robertbrault.com/2009/05/thoughts-of-hope-and-rejuvenation.html.
2. Francis Chan, *Crazy Love: Overwhelmed by a Relentless God* (Colorado Springs: David C. Cook, 2008), 112.

3. Tim Kizziar, quoted by Francis Chan, *Crazy Love*, 92.

4. See http://www.familieswithpurpose.com/how-to-use-family-mission
    -statement.html.

5. Adapted from Larry Forthun, "Family Nutrition: The Truth about Family
    Meals," *EDIS* (the Electronic Data Information Source), University of Florida
    IFAS Extension, Publication #FCS8871, http://edis.ifas.ufl.edu/fy1061.

CHAPTER 9: I'M NOT GOING TO LIE—DOING GOOD IS HARD

1. Mark Galli, "Insignificant Is Beautiful," *Christianity Today*, October 28, 2010,
    http://www.christianitytoday.com/ct/2010/octoberweb-only/52-41.0.html
    ?start=1.

CHAPTER 10: POWER OF ONE

1. See http://www.theworkofgod.org/Saints/Lives/MTeresa.htm.

2. Quoted in Gordon Geddes and Jane Geddes, *St. Mark's Gospel* (Oxford,
    England: Heinemann, 2001), 83.

3. See http://www.values.com/inspirational-quotes/4121-Stay-Where-You-Are
    -Find-Yo-.

4. Katie Davis, *Kisses from Katie* (Brentwood, TN: Howard Books, 2011), from
    the foreword by Beth Clark.

CHAPTER 11: JUST ANOTHER RICH MOM

1. Giving What We Can explains their calculations on their website. "You might
    think that the above figures are distorted because each dollar goes further in
    impoverished countries. However, we account for this: incomes are compared
    in terms of how much money is needed to buy locally what $1 buys in the
    United States." See http://www.givingwhatwecan.org.

2. Anup Shah, "Poverty Facts and Stats," *Global Issues*, last updated January 7,
    2013, http://www.globalissues.org/article/26/poverty-facts-and-stats.

3. See http://www.givingwhatwecan.org.

4. Steve Saint, "Projecting Poverty Where It Doesn't Exist," *Mission Frontiers*,
    September 1, 2011, http://www.missionfrontiers.org/issue/article/projecting
    -poverty-where-it-doesnt-exist.

5. "Americans Spent over $53 Billion on Pets Last Year," *Yahoo! News*, Associated
    Press, February 22, 2013, http://news.yahoo.com/americans-spent-over-53
    -billion-204113115.html.

6. Kevin DeYoung, "Getting to the Root of Radical: A Review and Response,"
    The Gospel Coalition: DeYoung, Restless, and Deformed (blog), May 25, 2010,
    http://thegospelcoalition.org/blogs/kevindeyoung/2010/05/25/getting-to
    -the-root-of-radical/.

7. Elizabeth Dreyer, *Earth Crammed with Heaven* (Mahwah, NJ: Paulist Press,
    1994), 23.

8. Jim Taylor, "Raise Children, Not Consumers," *Huffington Post*, September 5,

2012, http://www.huffingtonpost.com/dr-jim-taylor/advertising-to-kids
_b_1854319.html.

9. Stephen Mansfield, *Never Give In: The Extraordinary Character of Winston Churchill* (Nashville: Cumberland House, 1995), 125.

CHAPTER 12: DEFEATING MY BIGGEST FOES

1. Sharon Begley, "How Moms Make a Difference," *The Daily Beast*, May 7, 2011, http://www.thedailybeast.com/articles/2011/05/07/parenting-the -science-of-how-moms-make-a-difference.html.

2. This definition of struggle is attributed to ultramarathon runner Danny Dreyer, creator of the ChiRunning and ChiWalking methods.

3. This was a response by David Platt to a review of his book *Radical* at Kevin DeYoung, "Getting to the Root of Radical: A Review and Response," *The Gospel Coalition: DeYoung, Restless, and Deformed* (blog), May 25, 2010, http://thegospelcoalition.org/blogs/kevindeyoung/2010/05/25/getting -to-the-root-of-radical/.

CHAPTER 13: START SMALL TODAY

1. A. W. Tozer, *God's Pursuit of Man* (Camp Hill, PA: Wingspread, 2007), 50.

ABOUT THE AUTHOR

KRISTEN WELCH grew up in a suburb of Houston, Texas. In the 1990s she attended a small Bible college, where she met her husband and graduated with degrees in Christian education and English.

For the first ten years of marriage, she worked alongside her pastor-husband in youth and children's ministry in Arkansas, New Mexico, and Florida, often writing her own curriculum and resources. During this decade, she endured the ups and downs of life. It wasn't until she became a busy mother of three that she began to blog about her life on *We Are THAT Family*. Over the years, Kristen has grown a vast following of moms who identify with her real, often funny, and always inspiring writing.

In 2010, Kristen traveled with Compassion International to Kenya on a blogging trip to write about poverty in a huge slum. That experience turned her world upside down, and as a result, she and her family founded a nonprofit called Mercy House Kenya. The organization funds a residential maternity center, operated by indigenous staff, that offers hope and a home to pregnant teens living in extreme poverty.

In 2011, Kristen wrote her first book, a devotional for moms called *Don't Make Me Come Up There!* She is also one of DaySpring's (in)Courage writers, a frequent speaker, and a regular contributor to LifeWay's *HomeLife* and *ParentLife* magazines.

Kristen's blog following continues to grow, and many of the readers financially support the work of Mercy House. When she and her family aren't traveling to Kenya, Kristen and her husband and their three children live in Texas, where they enjoy going to football games and flea markets and trying new restaurants.